Black is the Journey,
Africana the Name

Critical South

The publication of this series is supported by the International Consortium of Critical Theory Programs funded by the Andrew W. Mellon Foundation

Series editors: Natalia Brizuela, Victoria Collis-Buthelezi and Leticia Sabsay

Black is the Journey, Africana the Name

Maboula Soumahoro

Translated by Kaiama L. Glover

polity

Originally published in French as *Le triangle et l'hexagone: Réflexions sur une identité noire* © Éditions La Découverte, Paris, 2020

This English edition © Polity Press, 2022

Reprinted 2022

Cover artwork: 'M. Angelou' | In 'The Malediction of Cham' series | 2020
             Painting, mixed media, 47 × 47 in
             Artist | Marielle Plaisir

Polity Press
65 Bridge Street
Cambridge CB2 1UR, UK

Polity Press
101 Station Landing
Suite 300
Medford, MA 02155, USA

ISBN-13: 978-1-5095-4832-3
ISBN-13: 978-1-5095-4833-0 (pb)

A catalogue record for this book is available from the British Library.

Typeset in 11 on 13pt Sabon
by Fakenham Prepress Solutions, Fakenham, Norfolk NR21 8NL
Printed and bound in Great Britain by TJ Books Ltd, Padstow, Cornwall

The publisher has used its best endeavors to ensure that the URLs for external websites referred to in this book are correct and active at the time of going to press. However, the publisher has no responsibility for the websites and can make no guarantee that a site will remain live or that the content is or will remain appropriate.

Every effort has been made to trace all copyright holders, but if any have been overlooked the publisher will be pleased to include any necessary credits in any subsequent reprint or edition.

For further information on Polity, visit our website:
politybooks.com

I dedicate this book to the late Dr. Colin A. Palmer (1944–2019), master of the diaspora, H.N.I.C. without parallel. In addition to the invaluable knowledge he imparted, he proclaimed me "Miss France" as of 1999. Astonished and perplexed at first, I was incapable of grasping the symbolic importance of this pronouncement until many years later. I have since held onto and taken care of that precious title. For this, I want to offer him my eternal gratitude.

Contents

With Naïma Yahi. Together, at the intersection.
Head held high.

"If it was up to me ...
It is up to me."
– Saul Williams, *The Wind's Song*, 1998.

Acknowledgments

My deepest gratitude to Natalia Brizuela, my editor at Polity Books, for her so precious warm, constant, and cheerful support and encouragement.

I would like to thank the Éditions La Découverte: Thomas Deltombe, Stéphanie Chevrier, and Valentine Dervaux, for their faith in me, their indefatigable support, kindness, and professionalism. The Centre international de recherches sur les esclavages et post-esclavages (CIRESC) at the CNRS (International Centre of Research on Slavery and Post-Slavery), directed by Myriam Cottias, kindly offered me a comfortable space in which to write this book. I am eternally indebted to it.

This work unfolds over and evokes three geographical spaces, adding a tricontinental dimension to my list of people to thank, necessarily rendered incomplete and necessarily diasporic. I offer my apologies in advance to those people and institutes whose names I may have omitted here, and have aimed to organize my thanks into two categories: "those who helped me to think" and "those who helped me to live (thinking all the while)."

Throughout the years, I have been invited by several universities to lecture on what was then still a project under construction. I would like to thank them warmly, since every such opportunity gave rise to feedback, remarks and suggestions, all of them wise, which contributed to the development of this work: Noëlle Rouxel-Cubberly (Bennington College); Madeleine Dobie, Kaiama L. Glover, Emmanuelle Saada, Shanny Peer (Columbia University); Astride Véronique Charles, Barbara Savage, Lydie Moudileno (University of Pennsylvania); Peter J. Hudson, Jemima Pierre, Robin D. G. Kelley (University of California, Los Angeles); Bernard Moitt (Virginia Commonwealth University); Pauline Guedj (New York University); Crystal M. Fleming (Stony Brook University); Cédric Moreau (University of Strathclyde, UK); Sabine Broeck, Carsten Junker (Universität Bremen, Germany); Nacira Guénif-Souilamas, Nadia Yala Kisukidi, Éric Fassin, Achille Mbembe (Université Paris 8 Vincennes-Saint-Denis); Ary Gordien, Ingrid Château, Ndeye Fatou Kane, Laura Khizar Hayat, Guita Nilavannane (École des hautes études en sciences sociales, EHESS).

I would equally like to note my great respect and gratitude towards all the professors, colleagues, and artists whose teachings, projects, productions, and intellectual exchanges nourished my thought in a lasting way: my mentor Ehiedu E. Iweriebor, Mark W. Payne, Joyce Toney (Hunter College, City University of New York); Judith Ezekiel (University of Toulouse/Wright State University); Édouard Glissant, Francesca Canadé Sautman (Graduate Center, City University of New York); Maryse Condé, Manning Marable, Abosede George, Kim Hall, Tina Campt, Samuel K. Roberts (Summer Teachers and Scholars Institute 2017), David Scott, Souleymane Bachir Diagne, Mamadou Diouf, James H. Cone (Columbia University/ Barnard College/Union Theological Seminary); Manthia Diawara, Michael A. Gomez (New York University); the "Interrogating the African diaspora" 2004 seminar; Jean

Muteba Rahier (Florida International University); Trica D. Keaton, Shatema Threadcraft (Dartmouth College); Janis A. Mayes (Syracuse University); Mame-Fatou Niang (Carnegie Mellon University); The Association for the Worldwide History of the African Diaspora (ASWAD); The Black Women's Intellectual History Project; Practicing Refusal: The Sojourner Project; The Berkshire Conference of Women Historians (Martha Jones, Tiya Miles, and Marisa Fuentes); Samir Meghelli (Smithsonian Institution's Anacostia Community Museum); Arthur Jafa; Zadie Smith; Léonora Miano; Jean-Éric Boulin; Kaoutar Harchi; Laurent Dubois (Duke University); Aaron Kamugisha, Jahlani Niaah (University of the West Indies); Stéphane Robolin (Rutgers University); Christine Chivallon (CNRS); Françoise Vergès; Elsa Dorlin (Université Paris 8 Vincennes-Saint-Denis); Omar Berrada (The Cooper Union); Alice Diop; Josza Anjembe; Nora Philippe; Penda Diouf; Bintou Dembele; Eva Doumbia; Rokhaya Diallo; Fabrice Taraud; Alexis Peskine; Rocé; Jon Soulclap; Cases Rebelles.

I particularly thank Bennington College and its extraordinary students; the Institute for Research in African American Studies (IRAAS, Columbia University), the Africana Studies department at Barnard College; Madeleine George and the students at Bard College Prison Initiative Program; my students at the University of Tours and at Sciences Po (Paris and Reims campuses), as well as all the prison residents with whom I have had the pleasure of working and from whom I have been able to learn so much.

My blood: my family (Soumahoro and Binaté), vertical, horizontal, extended (Mungani, Cottrell, Monnier, Hall, Moderne, Églantine), continental and diasporic, constitute the bedrock by which I have had the good fortune and happiness of being supported. I thank each member of our three generations engaged in this French experience. You are everything to me: the ground and the source. Massiami, Mahbintou, Monmian, Namisata, and Myriam, there are no more precious sisters than you. Naomi, Ismaël, Iman, Soheïla, Lana, Diane, Rémi, Kayla, Lola, and those to come: over to you!

Finally, I have been fortunate enough to be able to dive at will into an ocean of friendships that accompany me, soothe me, and support me in every endeavor. A huge thank you to the following people: the Fellowship of KB (Véro; Yoyo; KK, my Grande Caille); la Tana de Soumangourou; Schnavel; Joce et Malia; Ibrahima "Ibou" Traoré; Karima Boussalem, Cynthia Tocny (twelve years too late!); Hadja; Pika; Otuawan; Jimmy; Jennifer "Shakita"; Chida; Samia; Max; Nono and our Boonies: Craig, Louloute, Mamao and even Smootchax!; Patricia and Elie; Magalita, Maï Lan and Naïs; Houaria Righi; Aïcha; Angela and Jahia; Diadia ("the Miami Pact" has been respected!); Mame (so much love …); Negroblaster; Dr. Jovonne Bickerstaff ("the right to write"; right?); Dr Caterina Pierre; the fantastic Dr Gay Wilgus (since 2002 …); Dr Ella Ben Hagaï; Aïda Sarr; Aurélie Hannoun; Sébastien Salbayre; Alain "Al" Mazars, Maryline, and Jaë; Anne-Laure Feron; Raaf Matière Première, Rim, Yasmine, and Nesrine; Rachid Djaïdani; the ever caring Aline Tacite, Zaharia Ahamada; Jean-Christophe Folly and Michaëla Danjé ("the Pedra Alta Pact" will remain in vigor until the new order, literally). To my favorite Idos: Cédric, Jacky, Yacine, Raphaele, as well as to their descendants. To Suzette Tanis-Plant and Emmanuelle Andrès, my "thesis sisters." To Rosie Gankey and Marius, Cavé Okou, and Fania Nöel. To Christian Eboule; Yassine Belattar; Chloé Juhel, Raphaël Yem, Stella Magliani-Belkacem; Randianina Peccoud (thank you for your support and continual faith in me); Ta-Nehisi Coates and Kenyatta Matthews. To the Palenne, Libar, Jean-Baptiste and Peraste families. And to the N'Dour-Sow-Bary, Kompaoré, Ouedraogo, and Martin families.

To Émilie Barret-Chevrel. To F.B.: "We make a decision and we stick to it," right? I'm trying. Still and always. Thank you to her.

Translator's Note

I have been in conversation with Maboula Soumahoro for more than 20 years. We met during our graduate studies at Columbia University, both of us then students of Guadeloupean novelist and intellectual Maryse Condé, both of us going on to become scholars and educators in our own right. I do not recall whether Maryse made any sort of concerted effort back then to bring us together beyond that first encounter, but a connection was made and it endured. It would be the point of origin for conversations and collaborations that have stretched over two decades and back-and-forth across the Atlantic, into classrooms and cafés, with students and with various publics, and now here in the pages of Maboula's extraordinary book.

That Maboula entrusted me with translating her francophone journey into the space of the English-speaking world was an honor and a responsibility I did not take lightly. The invitation to translate her words into new places has felt, in a way, like a call to inhabit her voice from the inside out – an invitation to say "I" in her name. Because as much as the two of us have been in dialogue over the past decades, *Black is the Journey, Africana the Name* remains very much an individual's story; it is the story of an "I" that has risked telling itself openly, that has risked the vulnerability of visibility. As such, this project has required a constant navigation of the space between Maboula's experiences (as a Black French woman of sub-Saharan African heritage) and my own (as a Black American woman of Caribbean heritage). This process of navigation itself expresses what I understand to be the very project of translating this book – that is, to facilitate Maboula's generous *relating* of her story as a means to *relate* across nation-language and other cultural borders.

If the original French text of *Le Triangle et L'Hexagone* boldly insists on the presence – and the right to presence – of a Black woman, her body, and her deep history within the French republican community, this translated work insists on the presence of Black France in broader diasporic understandings of blackness within the global community. It insists that US-blackness cannot stand in for the experiences of the wider Black world. It brings us fully into the frame of a diasporic context that is geo-culturally idiosyncratic and deeply familiar, in equal measure. It offers readers in the Anglophone world an opportunity to see the workings and the consequences of racialization through a different lens and, in doing so, to understand both Frenchness and blackness in new ways. As the deliberately rare footnotes reveal (and then only in part), there are specific cultural codes and layers of reference that speak directly into the Francosphere but require the mediating work of translation in order to be legible to non-French readers. To be a Black woman in France is a particular valence of being a Black woman in the world, Maboula affirms; it implicates a particular history and is laden with a particular set of struggles. At the same time, the experience of Black womanhood we discover in *Black is the Journey, Africana the Name* is capacious. Maboula's intellectual engagements with racialized communities in

France, the United States, and the Caribbean, as well as her own facility with the English language, ground the diasporic resonance at the heart of her work.

"This question of language," as it is posed in the book's first pages, is troublesome. "This French language is not my mother tongue," Maboula flatly notes. "French is my mother tongue, though it is not my mother's tongue." Indeed, French is deeply fraught; Jula is painfully inaccessible; and English somehow resembles freedom in this particular story. If Frantz Fanon is right – if it is true that "to speak a language is to take on a world, a culture"[1] – then where does that leave Maboula Soumahoro, a Black French woman, born in Paris, raised by a Jula-speaking Ivoirian mother, most at home and most herself in New York City, speaking English? How does this "Black, transnational, diasporic identity" line up with her phenotype, her possibilities, her passport? What is the truest language of her story?

These questions are posed in ways both myriad and direct throughout *Black is the Journey, Africana the Name*, and they necessarily undergird my translation of this book from French into English. Rendering the eloquence and the adamance of the work's original prose, its provocative querying and insistent calls for reckoning and recognition, has required a uniquely intimate mode of engagement as a translator. It has offered me the privilege and the pleasure of dwelling deeply with and learning from Maboula's rigorously intellectual and insightful chronicle. It has meant journeying, admiringly, alongside her while striving to relate her words in my own mother tongue.

Kaiama L. Glover

Foreword

Saidiya Hartman

An autobiography of reading, observes Dionne Brand, offers the possibility of troubling the terms of being and the social arrangements produced by colonial texts and antiblackness. *An* autobiography embraces multiplicity, serial and collective iterations of Black life and becoming, in contrast to *the* autobiography where the definite article identifies "the subject to be made through colonial pedagogies" and the imposed plot of development and belonging. "An autobiography gestures to the world of a reading self," writes Brand.[1] The open question is how might acts of reading trouble, if not topple, the subject, the plot, and the world created by slavery, capitalism, and coloniality. Maboula Soumahoro's *Black is the Journey, Africana the Name* is an autobiography of reading, a critical memoir that also gestures to a self shaped and created by reading practices, more specifically, a self engendered by diaspora literacy.[2] Black study, as elaborated here, is not confined to matters of curriculum or the reading list, but is an embodied practice and a labor of the heart. The memoir, crafted through an extended set of textual encounters, is an account of linguistic estrangement and

chosen blackness. Soumahoro's autobiography of reading
engages a range of thinkers and texts, most notably Aimé
Césaire, Maryse Condé, Frantz Fanon, Yaa Gayasi, Paul
Gilroy, Edouard Glissant, Stuart Hall, Audre Lorde, Paule
Marshall, Achille Mbembe, and Léonaro Miano, in expli-
cating the history of the Triangle, the symbol for the three
continents involved in the transatlantic slave trade and
colonialism. These writers have provided a critical lexicon
for understanding blackness and diaspora, a knowledge
suited to the dimensions of the *tout monde*, and their
imprint on this work of autotheory is indelible. Among
the central questions of this text: What is the relation
between lived experience and the production of ideas?
What language is best able to convey the Black presence
in France? What justifies the use of the "I" in scholarly
work and critical theory? The text wrestles with these
questions at the level of form and proposes an answer in a
journey through a world of ideas and across the space of
the Atlantic. The "I" of this critical memoir is forged by
transatlantic histories and Black geographies.[3]

Black is the Journey, Africana the Name traces
Soumahoro's development as a young woman of African
descent in France, and the belated recognition or embrace
of Black identity in the French Hexagon, a context which
makes nearly impossible any understanding of her position
in the world or her daily experiences as a Black girl growing
up in the *banlieue*. The brutal incommensurability between
the routine violence of racism and the seeming neutrality
of the discourse of universalism and color-blindness thwart
any effort to think or address the processes of racialization
and enclosure in the metropole, let alone undo them.
With disavowal and blindness as the official mandate of
the nation-state, Soumahoro endeavors to find a way of
naming the self and narrating her experience in defiance
of the imposed terms (of impaired citizen and not-quite
French); she is unwilling to be silent about the forms of
address that imperil and disfigure Black life or the racial

reason cloaked as education and graduate training. This lucid and impassioned book attempts nothing short of dismantling the master's house.[4]

A journey of dispersal and gathering might be the best way to describe Soumahoro's reckoning with the histories of the Black Atlantic and African diaspora. *Black is the Journey, Africana the Name* recalibrates the conception of diaspora by amplifying the presence of Africa in the diaspora, not simply as origin, but as haunted and disfigured by the millions gone or lost to the slave trade, by the graves without bodies. The text embraces a language of blackness, which is figured by histories of struggle and emergent solidarities across the globe. It is an autobiographical example of the forces of dispossession and racialization that have produced the diaspora, as well as the exigencies and predation of capital, the interminable and recurring wars, and the longing for the good life that continue to expand and reshape the contours of blackness. This insightful and persuasive meditation on the meaning of the terms "Black," "Africa," and "diaspora" explores the legacy of transatlantic slavery, racialization, coloniality, and impaired citizenship.

The book is less interested in providing an overview of this history, than in attending to the character of Black existence in the contemporary world. It situates France firmly within this history of slavery and coloniality, yet this history is disavowed and whitewashed in the republic's instrumental deployment of universalism and fidelity to Reason. The significance of colonial slavery for Blacks across the globe was that it "inscribed a new sociopolitical order on the body." Soumahoro deftly attends to the burden of racialized embodiment. To have a body is to be tethered to the world and assigned a place within it, to be condemned to the lowest rung in the vertical hierarchy of human life. These histories of slavery and coloniality are written on the body, lived in the present, and traverse the diaspora, establishing relations across the Atlantic (even when this relation is defined by misunderstanding and friction, what Brent Edwards describes as *décalage*, "the joint is a curious place, as it is both the point of separation and the point of linkage").[5] These histories and their repercussions are shared in the Triangle and in the world, even as they are lived differently. They have produced the shared features of Black life in the modern world and bridge seemingly diverse formations. We are all living in the wake of slavery.[6]

In her journeys across the Atlantic and graduate education in the US, Soumahoro discovers a body of critical thought and literature, a frame of reference for understanding the histories and structures that make Black lives precarious and disposable in America, Europe, and Africa, a conceptual toolbox capable of perceiving and attending to the Black presence in France. This detour through the US and the history and literature of Black life in the Americas leads Soumahoro to claim blackness – she became Black of her "own volition." Soumahoro's retracing of the Triangle and the journey from the French metropole to New York City, a reverse journey of the Black Americans who traveled to Paris in the hopes of escaping racism, is a detour, an indirection that allows her to engage critically the situation of Black Europe at the level of generality. "The detour," as Glissant writes, "is the ultimate resort of a population whose domination by an Other is concealed: it then must search elsewhere for the principle of domination, which is not evident in the country itself: because the mode of domination (assimilation) is the best of camouflages."[7] This indirection, according to Brent Edwards, can indeed be "strategically necessary in certain conditions."[8] It proves to be essential for Soumahoro. It makes possible the production of "a common elsewhere" shared by the Black world. Glissant writes that "detour is not a useful ploy unless it is nourished by return: not a return to the dream of origin, or the immobile One of Being, but a return to the point of entanglement from which one was forcefully turned away."[9] Soumahoro confirms this. As she writes: "The detour had proven necessary, fundamental. It had been a matter of distancing myself in order to return. It had been a matter of distancing myself in order to return under better circumstances – by putting an end to all that had been silenced, or unconsidered when it came to race. After ten years, my return to my homeland was complicated" (p. 60). Soumahoro returns to the point of entanglement, her natal land, the place that denies her blackness and stigmatizes it, anchoring her in a body perpetually inscribed as a stranger.

For Soumahoro, the meaning of diaspora is one of expanding and overlapping multiplicities – a rhizomatic network affiliating Africa, Black Europe, and the Americas. There is a Black diaspora and there is an African diaspora. The former is articulated through histories of slavery and dispossession, coloniality and relentless acts of resistance; the latter circles round and gestures toward Africa presented as an ideal, historical origin, point of departure, lost homeland, and figure for imagining a future life, an anticipated freedom. This Africa is the vessel for emergent and realigned sociality and radical possibility. Even those with immediate natal claims and for whom this intimacy or relation might be taken for granted as a matter of fact dream of Africa. Both the terms "Black" and "diaspora" yield to possibility, or, at the very least, bear the potential for a different grammar of futurity,[10] a questioning of given narratives of origin and belonging, a detour from national citizenship and territorially bounded community.

Black is the Journey, Africana the Name is a memoir of intellectual formation as much as it is a work of criticism and theory. Its subtitle might easily be: "the crisis of the Black intellectual inside the French university," given the obstacles and impediments intended to thwart questions of race and racism in France and redirect Soumahoro's course of study. How can one think critically about blackness in a context in which such analysis is interdicted? In order to engage in the project of Black study, Soumahoro was forced to cross the Atlantic. While enrolled at Columbia University and the City University of New York, she studied with Maryse Condé and Edouard Glissant and, for the first time, read Black thinkers and writers from around the world in her university courses. This journey across the Atlantic and a decade of dwelling in New York cultivated the embrace of a transatlantic Black identity, a diasporic identity, which she encountered on the pages of critical and literary texts and in the streets of the global city. This transatlantic roaming and dwelling was a productive detour. This decade of study challenged and expanded her conception of blackness and diaspora and provided much needed critical tools to think the specificity of her condition as a Black citizen of France, a task that was difficult if not impossible inside France. As a result of this education in Black Studies, Soumahoro was able to disenchant the discourse of universalism and read the Black presence in France in a radically different register.

This knowledge of diaspora informs Soumahoro's refusal of the prevailing terms and the imposed language of color-blindness and its abstract yet exclusive Frenchness. Exclusion and anti-blackness are hidden behind the mask of the "universal." Rather than cling to the promise of disembodied citizenship, or enshrine it as an aspiration, Soumahoro takes for granted the fact that Black people are French citizens. It is not an esteemed gift for which the Black population of the metropole must prove worthy. As she writes: "This belonging to the French nation is not a diploma, not even a reward or a point of pride: it is simply a matter of fact" (p. 89).

There is the fact of French citizenship and there is the choice of blackness. The claim to blackness entails a politics of affiliation, a "conscious entry into a transnational community defined by its literary and artistic production, its spiritual practices, and its firm anchoring in intellectual traditions" (p. 90). While the racialization of population in the context of capitalism and colonial slavery has divided life into categories of the human, the not quite human, and the not human,[11] blackness transcends this hierarchy. It is more than fungible life and dispossession; rather, it entails relentless acts of resistance, refusals of the given, and conjures other visions of the world. It provides a guidepost for those in search of a language capable of illuminating the condition of the marginal and the wretched, the stranger in the house, those bereft of a mother tongue.

> French is my mother tongue, though it is not my mother's tongue. Might France be my mother? ... This linguistic gulf, result of a displacement, a migration, themselves echoes of a far longer history of displacements and migrations – might it reveal something about a vision of the world and of global history that are somehow incarnated in my Black body, moving through a society that claims to be blind to race? (p. 16)

This autobiography of reading is also an account of linguistic estrangement. The question of a mother tongue is as pressing for Soumahoro as any other Black writer in the diaspora, and she is as intent on finding an idiom, a tongue that might liberate her from the colonial script, from alienation and estrangement, from being a foreigner in her natal land. Unlike her parents, Soumahoro doesn't speak Jula or any other African language. Her first language is French, yet the language in which is she is most proficient feels foreign on the tongue. It is the constant reminder of her displacement in diaspora; it is the linguistic register of her dispossession and anguish.[12]

Perhaps the great surprise of the text is that English proves to be the language that makes it possible for Soumahoro to write blackness into being and to feel comfortable inside her skin. From the space of exile, or in the movement of the detour, Soumahoro writes diaspora by reimagining Africa, not as a given or as an origin, but as a territory of loss and longing for Black Europeans separated by only one generation from the continent. Imagination creates the shared sentiment of diaspora and remains its common language, not a mother tongue or its comforts. This observation is made plain in an itinerary of reading that includes writers from across the diaspora, all of whom are struggling to find an idiom to write Black becoming, Black existence across time.

How does one write as a "dominated person in a dominant country"? How does one create dangerously in an imposed language, in a mother tongue that is alien? How does one write in a state of dispossession? Does the "burden of race" differ, or is it intensified, when the instrumental language of universalism thwarts any and every attempt to speak to racism and antiblackness? Can the matter of blackness ever become indigenous to French soil, ever part of the national accounting? Is the status of the Black as perpetual foreigner and eternal alien ever to be eradicated?

After a decade of residing in New York City, Soumahoro returns to France. The journey back is difficult, yet she is able to find home in the soundscape of the Black city-within-the-city, in rap music and the contemporary hip-hop scene, perhaps the only space in the public sphere willing to engage the ugly history of the republic and avow the racialized order. It is the sole discourse available for representing the lives of those residing in the *banlieue* and at the margins of the nation. Only hip-hop artists seem capable of "conjur[ing] up the existence or the presence of Black French people within the space of the Hexagon" and without a detour through Africa or the Americas being required. Elsewhere, the fact of one's Frenchness is challenged and contested on every front. Black French are represented as outsiders to France. "No rootedness in Europe seems to be imaginable" (p. 81).

State violence and police brutality hone this sense of blackness and chosen affiliation; this enhanced vulnerability to violence and premature death is a condition distributed across the Atlantic. In 2005, the riots in the *banlieues* of Paris and other French cities and escalating police violence prompt Soumahoro to write her first article about France. "It became no longer possible for me to hide behind Black Americans to understand the functioning and consequences of racial categorization. It had become necessary for me to confront – to face up to – my own experience in my native land. Turning a blind eye had become impossible" (p. 69). It was the year the "race question" became a matter of public debate.

The burden of always having to explain the Black French presence by way of analogy or through the detour of the US or the Caribbean or Africa is no longer productive and quite damaging to the discussion of racism in France. The "exhausting task of explaining, translating and rendering intelligible situations that are violent, discriminatory or racist" is a task identified by Soumahoro as "the last detour" (p. 83). It goes without saying that the effort to explain has changed little despite the centuries of explanation and demonstration. "What is there left to understand? What remains so difficult to grasp?" (p. 83). Why the need to restate and explain the obvious: racism exists and it determines social, political, and economic relations. The violence of racism is "magnified tenfold by the denial of the very existence of racism." As Soumahoro writes:

> We are dealing with a powerful form of denial or with disavowal. If it is simply a matter of denial, one wonders what kind of pathological irresponsibility has prevented a coming to consciousness … we are talking about a conscious rejection of reality. The essential question is, then, to know what is hidden behind the relentless and determined denial and rejection of the reality of race. What, that is, is the point of refusing race? This relentless denial and rejection of reality is what exposes the very stakes of that reality (p. 84).

Black is the Journey, Africana the Name is necessary reading, now more than ever, as has been made clear by the protests against racism and state violence by millions across the globe. It is a powerful and eloquent book that expands our understanding of racism and writes trenchantly about blackness in a global frame.

Introduction

Black Speech/Speaking Blackness

> "I'm Blak with 7 k."
> – Chi Ching Ching, *One Knock*, 2011

As a daughter of the French Hexagon[1] and the Atlantic, my ancestry, my origins, my trajectories, and my own history inscribe me within the cultural, political, and intellectual vastness of the Black Atlantic, a geographic space deeply shaped by History. I want to talk about this space, characterized as triangular, that has brought together three continents – Europe, Africa, and the Americas – in ways both unprecedented and enduring. This space encompasses the Ivory Coast and Africa, my parents' homeland, as it does the French Hexagon, my birthplace, and the place where I currently reside, after having spent many years on the other side of the Atlantic, which is where I developed intellectually. Each of these spaces has, of course, its own particular way of reading both the Black body and the Black experience. I offer my own here. In dialogue with both the "big" and the "small" histories, as well as with the intellectual, artistic, and political traditions of the Black/African diaspora.

On diaspora

It is important to establish a frame, to set some parameters. We want to be clear on what we are speaking about. In fact, we *must* be clear on what we are speaking about. Words, terminology – they have meaning. And sometimes it is a good thing to go back to their original definition. Precisely so that we may know what is at stake.

As concerns the African populations dispersed across the globe, these days we use the term *diaspora*. This diaspora is generally described as "Black" or "African," according to the perspective we mean to emphasize. As such, to use the term "Black diaspora" is to foreground questions of "Black" skin and phenotype – the "Black" body, that is, its constructedness and its meaning – from the time when the African continent and Western Europe entered into what historians call the modern era, which now dates back just over five centuries. While this entrance into the modern age may have happened simultaneously, it certainly did not unfold as an egalitarian process. I am referring to Western Europe's colonial project, which began at the end of the fifteenth century and gave rise to exploration and conquest, and to the subjugation of peoples considered barbaric and seen solely through the prism of a preordained radical otherness – whether these peoples were encountered in a given site, as were Native Americans, or transported to new conquered territories, as was the case in the transatlantic slave trade. In such contexts, history, culture, religion, education, and the law each had a hand in fashioning Black life and Black bodies. These bodies evolved within highly hierarchized societies, where they sat at the very bottom of the social, political, and economic ladder. The Black body and Black life thus had to be understood as synonymous with inferiority. As a result, the term "Black diaspora" is used to insist on the importance of skin color and phenotype, and on the weight of social, political, and cultural constructions. It is not a matter of essence or biology, but of manufacture and construction.

When we use the term "African diaspora," it serves to emphasize the origins of peoples who are contained within that designation. Africa, as a continent, is crucial to matters of identity, though primarily as a point of departure and, at times, of longed-for, materialized, or fantasized return. Association with this continent, rendered inferior throughout history, undergirds the connections that exist between Africans and Afro-descended peoples throughout the world. From a Pan-African perspective, the fate of the diaspora is intimately linked to that of the continent. None can distance themselves from the continent of origin, deny it, or refuse to claim it: this would do nothing to change the fate of individuals or of the collective. Africa is engraved on the bodies, cultures, and history of Africans and Afro-descended peoples. We have to make do. Because the world makes do.

To speak of diaspora means to speak of dispersal, fragmentation, estrangement, and globalization. But to speak of diaspora also means to speak of connections, reconnections, admixture, creativity, and resistance strategies. The notion of diaspora, as it was applied to Israel and to the Jewish people, effectively implies that dispersal comes on the heels of catastrophe. We know only too well the catastrophe out of which originated the dispersal of Bambara, Wolof, Peul, Igbo, Yoruba, and other ethnic groups: the legal trade in human beings who came exclusively from the African continent. Those people were first moved to European countries before being transported *en masse* to the Americas to replace the decimated or disappeared native populations. In this place the Europeans called the New World, it was crucial to exploit the abundance of land to the maximum. It was crucial to generate colossal riches and to ensure that these riches benefited individuals, private companies, and entire nations. At least 12 million Africans were displaced in the context of this triangular trade, which took place from the fifteenth to the nineteenth century, bringing three continents – Europe, Africa, and the Americas – into contact in a fundamentally violent way. This figure – 12 million – does not take into account those individuals who died during the raids carried out in the interior, or along the African coast, or in the forts where the enslaved were held, first as they waited for the slave ships headed for the dreaded Middle Passage and then upon arrival in the Americas. Therein lies the question: how do we account for the number of people directly or indirectly affected by the slave trade? I am referring to a form of commerce unprecedented in the history of humanity. For if slavery has long been practiced by many human populations and has existed everywhere on the planet (to this day), colonial slavery is the sole form of enslavement that inscribed a new sociopolitical order on the body. That order revealed the identities of both Blacks and whites, created simultaneously and in maximal opposition.

Now that the frame has been established, we can turn to the manner in which individuals who have been constructed as inferior have made their way through societies founded on inequality. We know that any system of domination, because it implicates human beings – be they inferiorized, minoritized, or dehumanized – is inevitably called on to confront strategies of resistance put into action by those most subjugated, most marginalized, and most violently affected by that system. This resistance has always existed and unfolds in ways both direct and indirect. These acts of resistance take place in all areas of society. Such contestations amount to these populations' radical affirmation of their humanity. For the groups and the individuals who implement them, these contestations are an unsparing declaration of equality. These forms of resistance and contestation punctuate the history of the entire diaspora and include those of the African continent itself. Whether it be a question of Queen Njinga's defiance in the face of Portuguese authority; the echo of the explosion planned and directed by Colonel Delgrès at Fort Matouba in Guadeloupe, heard throughout Black America and preserved in its memory; or the luminous revolt of the enslaved of Saint-Domingue, which gave birth to the world's first Black Republic – a Republic that, in the space of an instant, gave true substance to the supposed universal ideals of the French Revolution of 1789. Whether it be a matter of the two victories of imperial Ethiopia in the face of Italy's colonialist assaults; the Rastafari awakening in Jamaica that produced reggae music, and whose international success unceasingly reminds us of the importance of grounded truths; or, for that matter, the Martinican sisters Paulette and Jeanne Nardal, graduates of the Sorbonne, translators and hosts of a celebrated literary salon, who laid the groundwork that allowed the monumental movement of Negritude to flower. Or, finally, whether it be a question of a French and Martinican psychiatrist, who, having been enlightened, joined the anti-colonial resistance in Algeria; or the victory of that very same Algerian nation in the face of France's arrogance and denial; or Diên Biên Phu;[2] or the group of women who declared themselves unapologetically "Black";[3] or an anti-racist march across all of France in 1983; or rap songs in French, one of which in particular describes France as a land where "the Fascists are furious and niggas ain't ready to face their fire"; or documentaries that persist in seeking out tenderness where its absence is expected, or in speaking up, projecting the bodies of Black Lady Liberties onto white screens.[4] These acts of resistance have been relentless.

What is this "I"?

I need to keep this simple. To get started by attempting to answer the fundamental existential question: who am

I? After that I can move on to developing an explanation of the way I situate myself within the French nation and the world in light of the rich history that has fashioned our societies, minds, and bodies. At stake is my ability to express myself in French in a way most apt to define and describe the spaces that will concern us here: the Atlantic world and the French Hexagon. The difficulties are numerous and may seem insurmountable.

"I have only one language and it is not mine." These words by Algerian-born French philosopher Jacques Derrida were chosen by French writer and sociologist Kaoutar Harchi as the title of her book, an analysis of the trajectory of five Algerian writers who chose to write in French. In her essay, Harchi explores the connections between literature and politics. This title interests me beyond the colonial question. Indeed, the question also arises in the postcolonial context.

"I have only one language and it is not mine."

This question of language, I also ask it myself. Born in Paris of parents who migrated from the Ivory Coast in the 1960s, my primary language, the one I use and practice the most, the one I know best, is French. So I should be able to call this French language my own, my mother tongue, my first or "natural" language. Yet this is not the case: this French language is not my mother tongue. It is neither the first language in which I expressed myself nor my "natural" language. Quite the contrary. For me, the French language is a language I acquired, albeit early on. As such, it is by no means a language that was transmitted to me "naturally" by my family, by way of my mother. Because French is not my mother's language. This is why it is difficult for me to clearly identify my mother tongue. I use the word "mother" here in its original sense, for I speak a language that is not that of my mother, one which I have been using since childhood, which is that of a country that itself is not entirely mine – the language of a country that has spread itself throughout the world. A strong country. A dominant country. A country of whose history I am one of the fruits. For this reason, between my mother and the French nation stands history. Between my mother and myself stands history. Between the French language and myself stands history. An ancient history, at once rich and complex, international, splendid and painful, silent, forgotten, or quite simply denied.

And yet, I exist.

And France is not my mother.

French is not, then, my mother tongue. And yet I am *also* French and I speak that language. And, again, it is the language I know and have mastered the best.

But this French language poses a problem for me. First, because it is not entirely mine. And then, because it does not allow me to express everything. To express everything I would like to express. In the silences of the French language, I encounter the heavy silences that at times stand between my mother and me when we speak in French. The silences that stand between us would be less frequent, I am very certain, if I could express myself in Jula. Jula is my mother's language. The Jula language does not belong to me either. I do not speak my mother's language. I speak a language that is not that of my mother. What does all this mean for me? How does it affect what I am able to say? What I am permitted to say? What I manage to express fully? Or not. I have found a solution to this situation and to these endless questions: I speak English. This allows for distance. The English language does not belong to me, it owes me nothing, and I owe it nothing in return. Things are so much simpler that way. I have loved this language since childhood; I learned it in stages, year after year, and ended up mastering it after much effort and many years of study. The English language has been so very practical for me. It bears none of the emotional weight that burdens both French and Jula. In English, I am free. I can express myself unfettered. I can reinvent myself. But in doing so, I create and establish new silences between France, the Ivory Coast, and myself. It is very difficult for me to express myself in French and in France on the subjects that I consider throughout this book. However, this is precisely the difficulty I hope to probe and to overcome. This will happen, inevitably, through the affirmation of my individuality within the context of an immense ensemble. And so, I must dare to say "I."

To embrace the pronoun "I," relying on the magic of a special dispensation, amounts to completely ignoring the classic injunctions of scholarly research. Hoping for some sort of emancipation and liberation, my conscious use of the pronoun "I" also signals a wholehearted claiming of individuality and a refusal to respect numerous and very serious protocols concerning the idea that critical distance must be maintained at all costs. In that respect, I renounce this so-called critical distance along with the notion of scholarly neutrality and objectivity; I remain indifferent to the accusation of non-rationality or of an inability to reason or analyze. For scholars, the pronoun "I" is absolutely prohibited. The human being, the individual, must disappear completely and thereby leave room for the purely intellectual, detached, disinterested, and disembodied. It is this last point I wish to interrogate. For my "I" is that of a Black woman who has evolved primarily between the French Hexagon and other territories of the Atlantic Triangle. For these reasons, my body cannot be erased from the equation. How could it be otherwise? The spaces in question here are those that fashioned this body that is mine and that, no matter where it is, is perceived as Black. And this perception has concrete consequences that themselves can only exist in direct contradiction with any intellectual claim to critical distance. Such distance is impossible for me. I do not even want it. I prefer a situated point of view, approach, and analysis. For the truth of the matter is, we are all situated. Personally, I simply do not have the luxury of being able to disembody myself and to think about the world, about society, or about people in a completely detached way.

This pointed use of the pronoun "I" requires, moreover, another form of courage and audacity. The courage and the audacity to finally dare to say "I" as one looks at one's own family, one's own life, one's personal trajectory, and, in so doing, brings together scholarly research and private, intimate experience. The courage and the audacity I refer to here require doing so in the context of the French academy and in the French language. For I am referring to a trajectory and an ancestry that are inscribed in specific historical periods, contexts, and geographic areas that plunge us inevitably and irrevocably into a particular French history: that of France's imperialist or colonial history, that of a racialized and racializing France, and that of a contemporary France whose status as a postcolonial Republic can be easily accepted, unlike its neo-colonial status, which also endures.

It is out of this combination of elements that the French title of this work emerged: *The Triangle and the Hexagon*. For me, it is simply a question of writing, publishing, speaking, and embracing these questions in France and in French, although for a long time it has been more comfortable, more practical, even, for me to pursue these Afro-diasporic reflections outside of France and in English – in other spaces, that is, also situated in the Atlantic arena, primarily the United States, but also the Anglophone Caribbean, where I have long felt freer, less paralyzed by the idea of thinking, formulating, developing, and completing this project. This feeling of freedom emerged out of my path through university, marked as it was by life-saving encounters that provided me with a more global approach to this Atlantic world. Given this, I must mention the centrality of courses by Édouard Glissant and Maryse Condé, scholars and writers who, though they were never awarded a tenured position in the French academy, built important careers in universities in the United States. I realize now that this ease and this freedom are in fact intimately connected to the deafening silence imposed by France, and to the impossibility – the illegality, even – of speaking about, naming, contemplating, or probing subjects, questions, and themes still considered unsettling to this day. These subjects, questions, and themes are nonetheless thoroughly mixed up in the great history that has transformed the space of the Atlantic and the rest of the world since the fifteenth century. This great history has produced, moreover, the forms of globalization within which we continue to exist.

In a context such as this, the personal and the intimate are intertwined with the political, the public. Being, then, of African origin, born Black in France toward the end of the twentieth century, my history and my journey are in fact inscribed in a history and in geographies far vaster than myself. That said, this history and these geographies weigh on and structure my life. Thus, in exploring them, in studying them, I explore and study myself. I become the subject of my own study. The question that presents itself, then, is what to do with this state of affairs. How am I meant to position myself? I suppose the answer implies a "coming out" of sorts, or perhaps what gender studies have defined as the indispensable precondition from which the individual situates herself politically, and in full acceptance of herself, within the society in which she lives. As far as I am concerned, I am a Black French woman. This part of my identity counts and will not be rendered invisible, neither in French society nor in French academia. This Black identity, because it is fundamentally political, inasmuch as it emerges from a wide range of historical processes, has of course been the subject of intellectual, political, religious, cultural, economic, and social consideration for centuries – specifically, as I noted earlier, since the beginning of the modern era. But beyond everything I have just mentioned, this Black identity has both implications and consequences.

I was born in Paris to Jula, thus Muslim, parents who left the Ivory Coast, a former French colony, during the 1960s. The reasons that led my parents to leave their native land are both banal and similar to those of people coming into France today – people that public opinion and the media have renamed "refugees" and "migrants." These reasons include seeking a better life by earning diplomas and seeking "a good job." I grew up in France, where I ultimately began a university education, which I then quickly pursued in the United States for more than a decade. There, I became fully conscious of the Atlantic world and of the historic diaspora within which my body was inscribed. In a global city like New York, my contacts with African-American, Afro-Caribbean, Afro-Latinx, African, and Afro-European people led to the forging of my Black, transnational, diasporic identity. Smoothly, with complete freedom and serenity. It was in the United States that certain answers came to me. It was in the United States and in the Anglophone Caribbean that I declared myself French and was believed. Lastly, it was in the United States that I was able to look differently at the Ivory Coast and Africa.

Now, you must not go thinking that I mean to paint some idyllic portrait of the United States and of the Americas, more broadly. That is far from my intention. The history of that country and of that continent has taught us all that nothing there is idyllic. Nonetheless, the Americas represent the original crime scene and the racialized space *par excellence*. The societies that developed there bring together all the populations that have played a role in modern history – all the racial and social identities that have been fabricated by history, be they dominant or dominated. Given this, there cannot be, nor should there be, any avoiding the matter of race over there. The case of France thus appears quite different, with its dichotomy separating the Hexagon from its numerous "overseas" territories, both former and present-day.[5]

I grew up in France in an extremely traditional Jula family that thought of France as no more than a temporary space of residence. I was raised with the myth of return, which, despite its specific links to that period in time and to the French context, seems to me to be quite similar, fundamentally speaking, to a number of such "back-to-Africa" projects developed by Afro-descended peoples of the Americas, violently dispersed and displaced by the transatlantic slave trade. I should add that this myth of return was by no means my parents' idea alone. It was also maintained by the Republic itself, which, in the years following the oil crisis of 1973 that ended the postwar economic boom, found itself counting on the departure of those it perceived as "migrant workers" – foreigners residing only temporarily in France. Neither immigrant nor worker during the 1970s–1980s, that myth of return, be it my parents' idea or that of the Republic, never should have applied to me. Yet both parties agreed about one thing: I was not French. It was not until the end of the 1980s that I obtained my first national identity card. This was when I began hearing about my "right" to French nationality by way of what the administration called "reintegration." This administrative jargon referred to the fact that my parents were born in the Ivory Coast at a time when that country was still a part of the French colonial empire. As such, I could be "reintegrated" into the French nation, as if some prior – some natural – order could finally be restored. As if Ivorian independence had been nothing but an exceptional parenthesis. But perhaps even more significant, these geopolitical considerations offered, to my mind, a concrete example of identity formation. In effect, my access to French citizenship is anchored in French colonial history. In my specific case, and this is the case for many others, the personal is political.

As concerns the way I was treated in France during my childhood, I can say that it varied considerably according to whatever vision France had on race, phenotype, skin

color, first and last names, religions, and social and
national belonging. In France I was perceived alternately
as Black, African, and at times Ivorian. My first and
last names were considered exotic. Islam, my parents'
religion, seemed antithetical to Christianity, atheism, and
secularism, all of which the Republic claimed to cherish,
though only sporadically. It also seems to me that being
Black and Muslim were seen as mutually exclusive. As if
one could not be both at the same time. As a Black Muslim
woman who does not wear a veil, I have never been
considered Muslim in France. Declaring myself so has
in fact raised great suspicion. Islam nonetheless enabled
me to make connections with numerous other African
communities from both sides of the Sahara. And lastly,
the question of social class also played a role, given that,
as a poor family, we lived in housing projects on the
outskirts of Paris and had the right to social services,
just like other so-called immigrant families more or less
recently settled in France. I am referring to Italian, Polish,
Yugoslavian, Spanish, Portuguese, Algerian, Moroccan,
Tunisian, Haitian, Indian, Vietnamese, Senegalese, Malian,
Congolese, or Cameroonian families. Along with these
families, there were some white French families and other
families from "overseas." Strangely, we all lived in the
same kind of place. And to a certain extent, our experiences were the same.

Only to a certain extent.

In 2016, I was particularly affected by a case of
police violence. It had to do with the excessively brutal
arrest of a young man named Théo Luhaka, from the
Aulnay-sous-Bois district in Seine-Saint-Denis. The fateful
encounter between the young man and the municipal
police ended with the former in the emergency room due
to an unspeakably obscene injury that to this day remains
unexplained. Beyond the fact of this sad but banal case of
police brutality, I was struck by its handling in the media.
In effect, during one of the televised debates that followed

Théo Luhaka's violent arrest, a representative of the police union declared that even if the officers implicated in the affair had called the young man a "bamboula," as the man claimed, that term, according to the union leader, was "still okay" to use.

How could I not react to the fact that the colonial origins of the term "bamboula" were left totally unexamined on the set of that television studio? It is crucial to note the specific character and the connotation of such an insult. In this particular case, using that specific insult goes beyond a matter of "mere" police violence, but has everything to do with racist police violence. The Théo Luhaka Affair and the debate around "bamboula" struck me in particular due to my first name, Maboula. In the Jula language, my parents' language, the feminine first name Maboula means: "she who opens the path" or "she who shows the way." I bear the first name of a paternal aunt who died before I came into the world. In my parents' eyes, as in the eyes of so many across the world and throughout history, it was a matter of preserving our lineage – genealogy based in repetition and homonymy.

The Théo Luhaka Affair and the debate that followed sent me right back to my French childhood, during which the sonic similarity between Maboula and bamboula made me – in the eyes of the French and of foreigners, of Blacks and whites – the unexpected incarnation of African savagery. For despite the vividness of an imaginary fashioned by the colonial period, even though that period was supposedly far in the past, a little doubt remained for most people. Perhaps it was true that the figure of the "bamboula" was not real; that it amounted to an odd, funny little fantasy that did not really exist. But upon meeting me, that subtle doubt would disappear. I was single-handedly the concrete and tangible incarnation of Africa and of Black being. The myth became reality through my own body. Through my own Black body. It was my body and my phenotype that ultimately gave full weight, meaning, and reality to the sonic similarity between bamboula and Maboula. There was no way around it. That is what I have come to understand only now. It explains why the kinds of debates I have just mentioned, be they intellectual or political, at times can resonate within me so deeply – within my flesh, within my psyche, and within my personal experience – and thus end up in my research. For it is always a matter of searching for meaning.

Even this first name and this body have taken on different meanings, depending on where I find myself in the Atlantic world. So it was that – long after the bygone days of my childhood, and those mass-produced Bamboula brand cookies or the children's game Dr. Maboul – an African-American human resources manager at the Graduate Center of the City University of New York library, where I was working at the time, told me how much she loved my name, which she found simply "beautiful." For the Jula, Maboula is a somewhat old-fashioned name these days. For other peoples of the African continent, it sounds "authentically" African. In Arabic, my name can be translated as "crazy woman," no matter what certain linguistic experts might claim to the contrary. And because certain Arabic words have passed into the French language as a result of centuries of both peaceful and violent encounters, "maboul" also exists in French and, if we are to believe our national dictionaries, the term is slang for crazy person. Through the Ethiopian prism of the Jamaican Rastafari, Maboula attests to my status as an African queen – never uprooted and pure of origin (never mind that I was born in Paris). For the Bushinenge from French Guiana, "maboula" is a cute, furry little animal to be domesticated and kept as a house pet. And lastly, in Paris, in an amphitheater at the Sorbonne during a colloquium concerning the Black/African diaspora, a white Belgian scholar of Negritude, before a packed room, turned my name into "Mamadou," thus suddenly and violently erasing in one fell swoop both my biological sex and my very gender identity – likely blinded, as she was, by her at once so logical and so longstanding perception of my body and of my phenotype. Every corner of the Atlantic had its own perception and its own vision of my body and my being, though they nonetheless remained unchanged.

And that's it for my autobiography. Autobiography matters because it allows one to situate things – to situate oneself and to make clear one's perspective. It should be mandatory across the board because it lays all cards on the table and, ideally, allows for conversation and exchange based in truth, reality, and good faith.

Universalism does not exist. It is itself situated.

The Hexagon is the land of my birth. French is my mother tongue, though it is not my mother's tongue. Might France be my mother? Might that be why I find it so difficult to explain things and ideas related to my actual mother? In other words, this linguistic gulf, result of a displacement, a migration, themselves echoes of a far longer history of displacements and migrations – might it reveal something about a vision of the world and of global history that are somehow incarnated in my Black body, moving through a society that claims to be blind to race? Such a vision of the world and of history make of me a Black woman within a society that is constitutionally color-blind. The problem, however, is that blackness and whiteness were born in the same historical moment. One does not exist without the other.

By way of conclusion to this introduction, I propose a quote from the novel *Homegoing* [French title: *No Home*] by the young Ghanaian-American prodigy Yaa Gyasi, which serves well to illustrate the objective of the study I am proposing here. The novel covers a historical period stretching from the eighteenth century to the present day. Toward the end of the novel, one of the characters, a man named Marcus, in an expression of what the Black American scholar Vèvè Clark calls "diasporic literacy" – that is, the fact of knowing how to read, decipher, and

write the Black/African diaspora – embarks on the writing
of a history thesis. He struggles to complete the project.
He is also unable to find the words to describe it to his
girlfriend Marjorie, of whom he is unknowingly a distant
relative. During a conversation about his thesis, Marcus
begins to ruminate:

> How could he explain to Marjorie that what he wanted to
> capture with his project was the feeling of time, of having
> been a part of something that stretched so far back, was so
> impossibly large, that it was easy to forget that she, and he,
> and everyone else, existed in it – not apart from it, but inside
> of it.[6]

1
The Triangle
Oxymoronic Circles

"But what if by beginning, everything came?"
Édouard Glissant, *The Fourth Century*

Chronotope

But the Hexagon is my birthplace. France is my fraught native land. Moreover, the term Hexagon poses a problem because it makes the mistake of referring uniquely to the European part of France. It renders invisible those territories that struggle – or even refuse – to integrate into it. Scattered throughout the world, notably in the Indian, Pacific, and Atlantic Oceans, this ensemble of territories dubbed "overseas" is material evidence that the Republic cannot be confined to its continental, European, Hexagonal dimensions. Indeed, the French Hexagon is inscribed fundamentally in a far vaster historical and cultural space: the Atlantic Triangle. Considered in its entirety, France is fully embedded in the triangular trade, and thus in a colonial and imperialist history. What, then, has this modern history put in place and deployed if not forms of racial categorization embedded in the body?

There is something paradoxical – ironic, even – about having recourse to mathematics, and to geometry in particular, as a means of thinking about the two spaces I have just identified: the Triangle and the Hexagon. As if there were no alternative other than to introduce a strong dose of rationalism, with the explicit hope of uncovering some logic in these two geographical-cum-historical spaces. As if only such a pure form of rationalism can be effective in granting the mind any sense of security in all this. This desire and constant quest for reassurance amounts, quite frankly, to a vain but entirely human attempt to compensate for, counter, or struggle against the inherent and fundamental movement, the unfathomable genealogies, and the at once troubling and chaotic timelines and histories of the Black/African diaspora.

In reality, the transatlantic diaspora that concerns me controls its own meaning, its own logic, its own orientations, its own functions, and its own splendors. As such, to study it requires no recourse to geometry. But I make do with the means at my disposal, even if that leads me to employ what might be interpreted, albeit wrongly so, as what Audre Lorde called "the master's tools." For let us remember that throughout history, the West has never been the sole producer of scientific and rational knowledge. For my part, I hope to dismantle the "master's house," whose existence simply cannot be denied. As for the existence of the master, that is, the figure of he who dominates, he must be acknowledged as such. Whether we say "master," "white," "male," "rich," Christian," "civilized," "heterosexual," "valid," "metanarrative," or "dominant discourse," each of these terms points us to the very same hierarchical political structures put into place by the West since the moment of its entry into the modern era.

Thus our point of departure must be at once chaos and the total acceptance thereof. It is a matter of the chaos of history, the chaos of secular displacements. This chaos has preoccupied scores of intellectuals, scholars, religious believers, artists, activists, and anonymous thinkers. But this chaos has not only preoccupied so many, it has also fashioned the practices of all those I have just mentioned. This chaos has also infiltrated the most intimate and most secret parts of my life. In effect, no matter how diligently I have concentrated all my efforts on identifying and conceptualizing new research tools, methods, and methodologies in an effort to explain, explicate, or rationalize the chaos I study, it never fades away. It persists. And no matter how fervently I pursue this vain attempt at elucidation, this so banal human desire to see through the opacity, it seems the solution may lie elsewhere. Perhaps we must recognize and accept both the permanence and the legitimacy of this chaos. It is based in rupture, invisibility, unspeakability, inaudibility, silence, and incessant movement. It is based in what is unknown and what is impossible to recognize or to know – in mystery, and in stories great and small. This chaos is based, moreover, in the complex roots and genealogies of narratives that have been produced and over which many battles have been fought. As for me, I strive to find meaning, some deeper understanding.

The diaspora that interests me takes place throughout the Atlantic Triangle, which British intellectual Paul Gilroy has named the Black Atlantic. This name has been contested, just as the very way we designate the diaspora has been contested. African? Black? On the one hand, to describe this diaspora as "African" attests to the desire to place the African continent at the center of all considerations. Africa is thereby acknowledged as the place of all departures and returns, successful or not. On the other hand, to describe this diaspora as "Black" attests to an emphasis on racial constructions and on the processes that such constructions underpin – based as they are on skin color and phenotype – at work primarily in the diaspora, but also on the continent. The idea would be, then, to focus on trajectories and flows rather than on roots and points of departure and arrival.

Another level of contestation around the term "diaspora" has to do with its legitimacy and applicability to African and Afro-descended peoples who, unlike other peoples, do not possess the necessary characteristics to enter into the closed circle of those more deserving of that status. But diaspora is neither a circle nor a status: it is merely the description of a reality. That of the dispersal of certain peoples across the world, even if works devoted to the subject reveal an overrepresentation of studies related to the history, memory, and cultures emerging from the Afro-Americas, to the detriment of studies concerning the actual space of Africa, as well as the Asian or European continents. Nevertheless, the situation is currently evolving, with work increasingly being done on those long-neglected spaces.

Since the first use of the term "diaspora" by historian George Shepperson in 1966, thinking about what constitutes the Black/African diaspora has been significantly enriched. The wide range of ideas about the phenomenon of diaspora includes the systematic study and comparative analysis of more or less geographically and historically proximate populations of Afro-descended peoples. The debates that have taken place in this field of study consider the question of the most fitting label for this diaspora – Black or African – as well as the matter of its usage in the singular or plural. Those who oppose the use of the term to designate the experiences of Afro-descended people dispersed throughout the world argue that there is insufficient cultural and historical unity among said populations, unlike the Jewish people, the Chinese, or the Armenians – populations whose diasporic status is widely acknowledged. The remarkable geographic and linguistic diversity of Afro-descended peoples would effectively disqualify them from inclusion within the category of diasporic. Specialists in Black/African diaspora studies have responded unanimously to this argument: the very diversity of places, languages, and cultures is precisely what constitutes the unity of those populations.

Scholarly and personal implications

What interests me are the transatlantic trajectories that have been fashioning Africa, Europe, and the Americas since the beginning of what history calls the modern age. The Triangle refers to the Atlantic, that geographic space strewn with the many migrations – voluntary, semi-voluntary, and completely involuntary – that produced the Black/African diaspora. My at once personal and professional interest in studying this diaspora is based fundamentally in a desire to make sense – to make sense out of that which is senseless or difficult to discern or to explain. That includes phenomena of chaos and inexplicable suffering as well as those of resistance and resilience. My research is about the analysis and understanding of dispersals, propagations, diffusions, crossings, and plans for return, be they real, imaginary, desired, voluntary or involuntary, successfully undertaken or not. I am interested in the Triangle. I am interested in the Atlantic world, which, at the beginning of the modern era, was the vector of the unprecedented linking of three continents: Europe, Africa, and the Americas.

My interest and my interrogations also have to do with my own relationship to this field of study. The introduction to the volume *Toward an Intellectual History of Black Women*, edited by Mia Bay, Farah Griffin, Martha Jones, and Barbara Savage, poses a crucial question in this respect: "What is the relationship between lived experience and the production of ideas?" More specifically, in the context of African-American or Afro-diasporic studies, what meaning can we give to knowledge production when one is both researcher and object of study? All kinds of feminists have already taken up this question, notably in thinking about the situation of the body. Discussion about the race-class-gender triumvirate emerged several decades ago. Since then, an awareness of sexuality has been added to the mix. Truly intersectional analyses continue to present a challenge in the present day. The level of complexity might certainly seem discouraging. *But Some of Us Are Brave.*[1] We find ourselves faced with an unavoidable imperative – that of relying on alternative sources and modes of scholarship. Identity and lived experience are central to these analyses because the objects of our investigation themselves exist at the margins of conventional and "legitimate" fields of study. Given this, we are brought to challenge, to redefine, and even to invent analytical categories. I would like to add the following questions to these considerations: at what moment and in what circumstances can personal lived experience become an intellectual object worthy of scientific query?

"What is the relationship between lived experience and the production of ideas?"

Am I an intellectual? Am I a woman? Am I Black? Am I capable of generating ideas? I effectively belong to all the categories I have just listed. My experience, my scholarship, the teaching I do, as well as others of my activities all bear upon my reflections, my research, and my politics. Because I consistently take part in Afro-diasporic intellectual conversations, it seems pertinent to me to look closely at how all of this is perceived in the Hexagonal context – which is both blind to the question of race – as well as at discussions of citizenship that result from this blindness. I am referring to the French republican space, its Hexagonal dimensions, that is, as a nation-state that, during the modern age, launched itself into imperialist projects along with all the other Western powers that spread themselves across the globe. The

Triangle in question here includes the Hexagon and places it within the wider context of a global Black identity that weighs on my personal experience and fashions the contours of my research. In this regard, I am very much indebted to Stuart Hall's theory, especially his reflections on "societies structured in dominance." Taking this idea as my point of departure, my vision of contemporary French Hexagonal society is as follows: at once post- and neo-colonial, the Republic functions as an ensemble of overlapping hierarchies of class, race, and gender. At its core persist a number of processes of racialization that have an effect on the whole of society. Whether they have a visible or invisible, favorable or unfavorable impact, these processes concern all members of the population, even if the dominant groups enjoy the privilege of invisibility and normativity. I will further add that for the last several centuries, we human beings have all been forced in very pointed ways to get used to seeing ourselves and others through the prism of race and phenotype. Though without any biological significance, these categorizations can have incredible power. They operate in very concrete social, political, and economic ways. Individuals, populations, and communities "of color" exist. To deny their existence and the injustices suffered by members of these communities is part of the current problem in France.

The theoretical and analytical tool proposed by the Black/African diaspora, given that I study this diaspora as a member thereof, has also allowed me to make sense of my own Afro-diasporic trajectory. As far as that is concerned, the question of my citizenship, of my full and complete belonging within the French nation, has become abundantly clear to me. But what do these notions of belonging and non-belonging actually mean? What does it mean to belong to a racial category or to a particular group? How do such feelings translate into my will to fight for greater justice and equality within the academy as well? What do I have the right to say or to write on

this subject? On what grounds? In what form? To answer
these questions, I propose a glimpse of the themes I work
on (and that work on me) and that must be linked to my
own transatlantic trajectory between Africa, Europe, and
the Americas. From the original departure of my parents
from the Ivory Coast to my birth in Paris, to my many
trips to the Americas, what might be my vision and my
experience of such notions as homeland as a point of
origin, of belonging, and of filiation? It seems necessary
to me to set off from the fundamental chaos of such
beginnings.

An intellectual tradition

I am fascinated by ideas of homeland and return, explicitly
linked to this fundamental chaos – this dispersal and
eruption – out of which the Black/African diaspora emerged.
On this subject, the writings of Maryse Condé and Saidiya
Hartman, as well as more recent work by Léonora Miano,
Ta-Nehisi Coates, and Yaa Gyasi, examine notions of
homeland and return each in their own fashion. Indeed, as
early as the 1980s, Guadeloupean writer Maryse Condé's
first novel, *Segu*, offered a meticulous and responsible
exploration of diasporic dispersal. One wonders whether
the writer, whose origins are sited on one side of the
Atlantic, was seeking to make sense of the original point
of departure that is the African continent. A veritable saga,
Segu examines the very first moments of dispersal through
its narration of the individual and collective destiny of
several members of a West African Bambara family.
Genealogy passes down through the masculine line.

Nearly three decades later, Yaa Gyasi's first novel,
Homegoing, presents a beautiful updating of the themes
and chronology of *Segu* via the genealogy of a pair of
sisters. As a Ghanaian-American, product and symbol
of African migration to the United States since 1965, the

young author proposes a new perspective on the diaspora. She brings to light the development and definition of African-American identity in the United States, insofar as, by virtue of their more recent and more concrete proximity to the African continent, these "new" African-Americans, a group to which Gyasi belongs, raise the question of what meaning to ascribe to the term "African" in the label "African-American." Yaa Gyasi's novel evokes themes of genealogy, identity, time and chronology, history, and the possibility or impossibility of speaking and narrating. In effect, how can one ever trace trajectories so deeply anchored in a complex combination of history and geography, both of which are incommensurably vast and indissociable, one from the other? And how can one address the issue of position? In other words, what might be the relationship of each individual to that history and to that ensemble of spaces in the present day?

Between the particularly notable respective publications of Condé's *Segu* and Gyasi's *Homegoing*, African-American scholar of Caribbean origin Saidiya Hartman has, in *Lose Your Mother: A Journey Along the Atlantic Slave Route*, reflected on what seemed to her to be the likely impossibility of truly recovering the African continent, seen to be the original or ancestral homeland for those whose ancestry is irremediably linked to the transatlantic slave trade. This work has been much debated and the subject of numerous controversies. In *Between the World and Me*,[2] African-American journalist and writer Ta-Nehisi Coates locates the African-American homeland squarely on United States soil – in particular in the cultural and educational enclaves that historically black colleges and universities (HBCUs) have fostered since the second half of the nineteenth century – despite the real interest he has shown in African and Pan-African cultures. Among these institutions, Howard University, situated in the US capital, is certainly the most prestigious. The author considers Howard his personal "Mecca."

Lastly, in *La Saison de l'ombre* [Season of the Shadow], which received the 2013 Prix Femina (the first time the prize has been awarded to a Black author), novelist, essayist, and playwright Léonora Miano deeply anchors her words and her writing in the African continent, as opposed to the diaspora. She gives Africa pride of place; it has the floor and must relate a painful story, at once current and long past. *La Saison de l'ombre* aims to speak both to the diaspora and to the African continent: the former must hear and understand experiences of suffering, while the latter must neither forget nor silence the troubling and mysterious disappearances that we since have come to understand. If the African continent remains at the center of Miano's concerns, it is Africa that must confront the initial misery of extraction and uprooting out of which the Black/African diaspora emerged. In this, Miano shows a rich historical knowledge of Afro-diasporic history and cultures. She insists, however, that what is hybrid and creative about the diaspora began on the continent, well before the departure toward what the conquering Europeans named the New World. Through her skillful handling of the phenomenon of exiled women and of the mystery surrounding the disappearance of young boys – the children of these women – as both point of departure and tipping point, the author carefully considers questions of genealogy and filiation, power and authority, silence, memory, and processes of creolization and acculturation. Embedded in this history, these ideas and processes relate the true History, with a capital "H."

The question raised by the ensemble of intellectuals I have just presented is one of beginnings. The beginnings of the diaspora. Where does it begin? Where and at what moment did the original take place? In the interior of the continent? Outside? Within both of these spaces? These legitimate questions oblige us to approach differently the vanishing frontiers, the fraught and problematic tempo-ralities. Did Edward Saïd not announce already that "the problem of beginnings is the beginning of the problem?"[3] As such, we are presented with a striking oxymoron: the circular nature of the Atlantic Triangle.

The challenge of telling these stories adds to that of writing them. In this regard, let us look more closely at Saidiya Hartman's *Lose Your Mother: A Journey Along the Atlantic Slave Coast*, which appeared in 2007. The book's structure is hybrid. It is at once a memoir, a work of ethnography, and the fruit of the reflections of an African-American scholar of Caribbean origin. Hartman tells the story of one of her trips to Ghana. She explores history to the same extent that she explores herself. Trained in literature and history, as a researcher she feels the absolute need to sound the depths of and relive the transatlantic slave trade as directly as possible. The archives are not sufficient: she must be on site and engage both her mind and her body in an experience that cannot be limited to conventional academic research. As such, in her role as historian, she visited the Ghanaian forts in which the enslaved were held captive prior to being transported to the Americas, and followed the path taken by enslaved individuals kidnapped from the interior and led to the coast, where those forts had been established, in the hopes of bringing together the spirits and the bodies of those who were enslaved, those who were displaced and dispersed, those who traversed the Atlantic, those who lost their lives along the way – voluntarily or involuntarily, within Africa or during the Middle Passage. In Hartman's eyes, academic research – cold, distant, ostensibly objective – proved insufficient. For among the historical archives dedicated to the transatlantic slave trade, few include any direct testimony by the children, women, and men who were enslaved. The stories and the history that has been written on the basis of those archives, whose scholarly value is acknowledged and accepted as constitutive of the academic discipline, can only reflect the version of the dominant group. The experience, the voice, the stories of those who were defeated, conquered, and dominated are completely missing.[4] As a result, how can one possibly hope to bear witness to this traumatic history across several generations and at a global scale if so much evidence and so many archives simply are not accessible?

This is a fundamental issue, in that it calls into question the very foundations of the academic discipline that is history. In effect, when it concerns the Black/African diaspora, the traditional academic approach reveals itself to be – de facto – absolutely insufficient and incomplete. Lacking archives produced by those most affected and without any recourse to the oral history of those individuals, given the centuries that have since passed, this specific history is transformed into a mere "memory" – that is, a sort of subdued history. A sub-history, a history infected by emotion. In other words, a non-academic history. That being said, faced with this order of things, the subterfuge uncovered by Saidiya Hartman takes the form of locating missing evidence and archives within the bodies of the descendants – the excretions, even – of those enslaved and scattered African populations. Thus do bodies and skin color amount to the sole traces, the sole indicators, the sole evidence, and the sole archives accessible in our time. This explains the extent to which any "return" to the original homeland and reconnection with the ancestral land prove nearly impossible in Hartman's eyes. A complete, unabridged testimony simply cannot emerge. On this point, Hartman declares:

I, too, was a failed witness. Reckoning with my inheritance had driven me to the dungeon, but now it all seemed elusive. I struggled to connect the dots between then and now and to chart the trajectory between the Gold Coast and Curaçao and Montgomery and Brooklyn. But I kept fumbling.

I could rattle off all the arguments about the devastating effects of having been property, denied the protection of citizenship, and stripped of rights of equality. The simple fact was that we still lived in a world in which racism sorts the

haves from the have-nots and decides who lives and who dies.
Racism, according to Michel Foucault, is the social distribution of death; like an actuarial chart, it predicts who would
thrive and who would not. Blacks are twice more likely to die
than whites at every stage of life and have shorter life spans.
In my city, black men have life spans twenty years shorter
than white men's, and the infant mortality rate among black
women rivals that of a third-world country. Blacks are five
times more likely to die of homicide and ten times more likely
to be HIV positive. Half of black children grow up in poverty
and one-third of all African Americans live in poverty. Nearly
half of black men between the ages of eighteen and twenty-
five are in jail, on probation, or on parole, and are four times
more likely to be sentenced to death than whites; and black
women are eight times more likely to be imprisoned than
white women.

The distribution of wealth is no less dire. Forty years after
the passage of the Civil Rights Act, black households possess
one-tenth of the wealth of white families; blacks own seven
cents for every dollar owned by whites.

This in part explained why I was in the dungeon. But
it was personal too. Hovering in an empty room was my
attempt to figure out how this underground had created and
marked me. Could I trace my despair back to the first generation stolen from their country? Was it why I sometimes felt
as weary of America as if I too had landed in what was now
South Carolina in 1526 or in Jamestown in 1619? Was it the
tug of all the lost mothers and orphaned children? Or was it
that each generation felt anew the yoke of a damaged life and
the distress of being a native stranger, an eternal alien?

I was loitering in a slave dungeon less because I hoped to
discover what really happened here than because of what
lived on from this history. Why else begin an autobiography
in a graveyard?[5]

This long extract from Hartman's work perfectly illus-
trates the whole of her project. All of it is there: past and
present, history and memory, freedom and chains, life
and death, wealth and poverty, men and women, adults
and children. Also there, however, is the general and the

particular, the interior and the exterior, that which belongs to the public sphere and that which belongs to the private – even intimate – sphere, the beginning and the end, light and darkness, death and rebirth, departure and return, unending quest and questions to which no satisfactory answer can reply, the quest, the mental anguish, the quest, loss, impossible responses, quest – diaspora.

In her work, Saidiya Hartman tells the story of a difficult, even impossible return to the so-called ancestral homeland. She points out its multiple points of tension. Among them, "Africans" who sold other "Africans" in an age when such peoples did not use this term to define themselves. Present-day Africans who seek to forget that painful past, but then are perfectly capable of recalling this painful past if it can be transformed into a lucrative industry based on "memorialist" Afro-diasporic tourism. Africans who are ready to benefit from this diaspora, so hungry to return to its homeland and to confront a past that is at once weighty and foundational, even though there is nothing to find but "shit and dirt and waste."[6] Present-day Africans are trapped in a disastrous geopolitical situation and face innumerable structural difficulties, unable to do anything but envy the African-Americans who, by contrast, incarnate the United States and the wealth of the West. In writing and describing all of this, Hartman also delves into Afro-diasporic language and culture – a diasporic literacy consisting of people, places, and events that resound across the diaspora and the world. Thus, evoking Kwame Nkrumah, James Baldwin, Bob Marley, the Ashanti empire, Samory Touré, Mary Prince, Walter Rodney, and many others, Hartman's writing and voice emerge from the diaspora. Both are situated outside of the distant continent of origin, a space so often imagined, idealized, desired, and fantasized as a place of refuge. Yet no refuge is to be found. Only the very end of the book offers some measure of respite. In effect, Hartman finds herself facing a group of little Ghanaian girls, standing in a circle as they play and clap their hands. Most likely because the scene recalls her own American childhood, this moment of long-awaited connection, however immaterial, contrasts starkly with the concrete effects of contemporary reality. And yet that is all that remains. All that is tangible.

In contrast to Hartman's bitter observations, a glimmer of hope seems to present itself in Léonora Miano's work. The Franco-Cameroonian author extols transatlantic, Afro-diasporic communication, along with the need to acknowledge the status of the African continent, not as the only but as the first victim of the transatlantic slave trade. Published in 2013, *La Saison de l'ombre* gives voice to Africa. The continent has to express itself in its own name. In this way it is able to join fully in a conversation that until that point has taken place almost exclusively in the diaspora. What exactly happened back in that time? To respond to that question and to the nagging doubts it contains, Miano proposes a fictional story centered around the Mulongo clan, struck by the disappearance of 12 of its young boys. The latter had temporarily left their village to take part in the traditional initiation rites that took place at their age. These lost boys had been chaperoned by two respected adults, both of whom also disappeared without a trace. Because the disappearance of these children and adults was unexplained and inexplicable, it was deemed mysterious, dangerous, and potentially a bad omen for the rest of the clan. The women – specifically, the boys' mothers – were the first to be cast out of the community. It was a question of taking all necessary precautions. The clan had to be prepared. The community had to be protected, even at the cost of marginalizing those who might just as easily have been considered the first victims of this collective drama.

The task taken up by Léonora Miano in *La Saison de l'ombre* is that of rehumanizing the history of the transatlantic slave trade. Miano quite literally gives life to the protagonists of a stretch of transatlantic history, one sought out – in vain – by Saidiya Hartman in *Lose Your Mother*. Here, it is literature that allows for a sort of relief in the face of a painful and necessarily incomplete historical record. Miano attempts to respond to the following question: what memory or memories does Africa retain of slavery and the transatlantic trade? According to the author, it is undeniable that the weight of such losses and mysterious disappearances has been, first and foremost, heaviest on the shoulders of African mothers, families, and communities. Only a few individuals, members of a powerful elite, had a global vision and true understanding of what was really happening. Only this elite profited from the unspeakable trade in human flesh. And still, no one could have fully grasped the consequences of this trade in the long term. Indeed, these very elites ultimately felt its terrible, irreversible effects. For Miano, Africa has retained the memory of these unexplained losses; of these empty graves without bodies to fill them that have made proper mourning impossible; of these annihilated and reinvented cosmogonies. Africa has retained the memory of all of this in songs invented, transmitted, and sung by its women and girls.

The question of return

The idea of homeland and return that punctuate the intellectual, political, and artistic traditions of the Black/African diaspora are of particular interest to me, given my birth in Paris and my Ivorian, Jula, Muslim parents. I must admit, however, that my interest was heightened once I began my own travels across the Atlantic Triangle on heading to the United States. At the time, the way I initially saw the two societies – French and US-American – took a happy, even life-saving turn. For example, when, in the Hexagonal context, I take up the task of exploring the imbrication of Black identity and the Islamic faith, I am well aware of the vast diversity among the numerous Muslim communities scattered throughout the rest of the Atlantic Triangle. In the specific case of the United States, it is crucial to make a distinction between, on the one hand, the African peoples brought there from geographic regions already under Muslim influence at the time of the Atlantic slave trade and, on the other hand, those African-American Muslim communities that emerged at the beginning of the twentieth century as explicit counterpoints to a dominant white Christian identity in the United States. For Noble Drew Ali's Moorish Science Temple of America or the Nation of Islam, it is a matter of individuals, groups, and communities who made the conscious choice to become Black Muslims. That is, people who made Black identity a religion and, in doing so, developed the notion of a Black God who has endowed demeaned Black populations with His divinity, humanity, masculinity, power, and legitimacy. Both a form of liberation theology and a dialectical process, the Black God is rendered human and Black people are rendered divine.

As for the Hexagonal context, it is a whole other story. In effect, the terms "Muslim" and "Black" seem to designate two completely separate categories. Both of these categories refer to racialized groups that are at times conflated. Thus, within the Hexagon, there exists a perspective on Islam that views the religion as a tool of racialization. In other words, if we follow the logic developed by Achille Mbembe in his theory of the "Negrification of the world," the Muslim is a Black man. He is, in fact, treated as such politically and socially. If we add in the gender question and the specific issues facing women, the function of the category "Black" becomes even more complex. In effect, the Hexagon tends to perceive visibly Muslim women as ambassadors for their chosen religion. These women are often discriminated against and stigmatized. They are depicted at once as problematic for being too visible in public spaces, and as vulnerable and needing to be saved from a condition imagined to be miserable and unwanted. These women must be protected by the Republic. These women's religion renders them incapable of Frenchness. Citizenship in this case implies abandonment of a religion that is itself a problem and that must be questioned. In the case of visibly Muslim men, they must be monitored, surveilled, and incarcerated. And for those who pose too great a risk to the security of the State, the penalty of death is almost automatically pronounced outside of any court – without much attention paid either to the nature or to the legitimacy of their faith. Be they men or women, these Muslims can be identified by their bodies, social or physical. That, too, is a form of blackness.

When I pursued my post-secondary studies in Hexagonal France, I chose to pursue my studies in English. At the Master's level, I specialized in the civilizations of the Anglophone world, at that time limited to the United States and Great Britain. I studied in particular the history of minorities in the United States and imperial Britain. Later, African-American and Afro-diasporic Studies became my fields of study. This specialization began with my work on the founding of Liberia. The history of the West African region that would become Liberia began at the start of the nineteenth century. The country is the fruit of a philan-thropic project initiated by the American Colonization Society in 1816. Among the members of this organization there were numerous men from the US South, some of enslaved persons and some not. After acquiring land situated on the West African coast, the organization began a colonial project that aimed to facilitate the "return" of free Christian Blacks from the United States. Deemed "civilized" because they had been Westernized and converted to Christianity in the context of the slave trade and the institution of slavery, these Blacks were meant to serve as veritable missionaries and, in turn, to "civilize" the local African populations.

At the beginning of the nineteenth century, the US-American slave society did not look well on the presence of individuals and communities of free Blacks on national soil. They constituted a threat to the country's socio-racial order: although free, they were Black and, as such, could not expect equal treatment from whites, rich or poor. The vast majority of the members of the American Colonization Society thus comprised fervent partisans of the "peculiar institution" who were in favor of the emigration of free Blacks. The latter could and should "go back to where they came from." And so, despite the concerted opposition of the majority of African-American political leaders and activists at the time, who were fighting for racial democracy throughout the nineteenth century, thousands of African-Americans volunteered to emigrate to what was said to be their land of origin. During the period preceding the US Civil War and the abolition of slavery that followed, these candidates for emigration were primarily Blacks who had lost all faith in the possibility of true equality between Blacks and whites on US-American soil. Ultimately, the colonial project implemented by the American Colonization Society led to Liberian independence in 1847.

What attracted me to this Americano-Liberian history – to this emigration project created for free Black popula-tions in the United States – was the appeal of African land, of Liberian land, in the collective consciousness of these African-Americans. Why and how did the African continent in general and Liberia in particular continue to function as a desired and idealized homeland – ancestral home and site of return – for people whose ancestors had left that geographic space centuries earlier? How did that fantasized elsewhere function within populations that occupied such a peculiar place among all the Black populations of the Americas that had been displaced by the transatlantic slave trade – that is, one of the most foundationally American Black populations, one of the most Creole American populations? In effect, the land that was to become the United States of America as of 1776 only received between 5 and 7 percent of the total number of Africans displaced from Africa to the Americas during the transatlantic slave trade. The United States had made the decision early on to encourage and to organize the natural increase of their enslaved populations rather than constantly import African slaves, as was the practice in the French colony of Saint-Domingue. It is well known that France's "pearl of the Antilles" paid a high price for this. But the subject that concerns us here is that of the notion of belonging to and anchoring in a land of origin – the at once imperturbable and unshakeable desire for a home. That is what brings us to the French translation of Gyasi's first novel *Homegoing*. How is it that the original title of the novel, *Homegoing*, which expresses the idea of a return home, concrete or not, was transformed in the French edition into *No Home*, a negation of the very existence of such a place?

My doctoral thesis allowed me to push further the work I had begun during my Masters studies by comparing two Black communities in the Americas: the African-American members of the Nation of Islam and the Afro-Jamaican members of the Jamaican Rastafari movement. Each of these communities emerged in their respective localities during the course of the first decades of the twentieth century. For both groups, reflections on God's racial identity and the religious, political, and economic consequences thereof was all-important. Given this, any hope for the complete liberation of Black people necessarily comprised a spiritual or religious dimension. My study also considered the context that preceded the emergence of each group, notably putting into perspective the central role played by the Universal Negro Improvement Association (UNIA) and its leader Marcus Garvey. It is undeniable that for thinkers like Marcus Garvey, Amy Ashwood Garvey, Amy Jacques Garvey, and the members of the

UNIA, all of whom had emerged from the Black nationalist and Pan-African militant tradition, Liberia was seen
as the privileged site of return for Black diasporic peoples.
Despite the historical conditions of its establishment,
Liberia was presented as the motherland. Once again, I
had to acknowledge the deep anchoring of the notion of
a lost but ultimately recoverable Africa in the imagination
of Black people of the American diaspora. Once again, the
desire for home was apparent.

The fruit of these initial research endeavors concerning
the creation of Liberia, political and religious Black
nationalism, Garveyism, the emergence of the Nation
of African-American Islam, and the Afro-Jamaican
Rastafari movement was the development of my intellectual interest in the Black/African diaspora of the
Americas and its relationship to Africa. The field of study
devoted to this diaspora, which functions via the prism
of history, geography, politics, and culture, considers
Afro-descended peoples and their regionalist or global
self-definition, independent of the borders that the nation-
state model has imposed. Relatively speaking, this field
has blossomed only recently. One of the primary pitfalls
facing scholars invested in this field has been the difficulty
of designing efficient tools and techniques that allow
for full and complete comprehension of the vast spaces
that make up this diaspora and the historical periods it
has traversed. For even if one tries to circumscribe the
Black/African diaspora to the Atlantic space alone, how
can researchers develop solid theoretical frames based
in the peregrinations of African and Afro-descended
peoples within this very space? On this particular point,
expert Ruth Simms Hamilton[7] has insisted on the circular
dimension of this diaspora, despite its emergence out of
a Triangle. The argument she proposes is as follows: it is
difficult to clearly identify both the points of departure
and points of arrival. The circularity she evokes here thus
highlights the almost complete impossibility of identifying

the definitive beginning and end of this diaspora. Thus, since the beginning of the modern age, the circulation of peoples, cultures, and ideas within the Atlantic Triangle is infinite.

2

University Trajectory

Atlantic Peregrinations

"Master the Ceremonies"
– Lunatic, "Intro" (2000)[1]

Black orbit

I have taught in the same university for the past ten years. I have also taught in the context of other institutions both in Hexagonal France and in the United States. This trajectory began overseas more than 15 years ago, and I shall attempt to decipher it now. It requires clarification that, I hope, will help me understand why this was such a fraught and difficult experience. Despite my meteoric social ascension. Despite holding a PhD in the study of the Anglophone world and my current status as a certified Professor and Lecturer in English. My education, primary and secondary, initially unfolded in Hexagonal France. I then went on to post-secondary studies in several French universities before pursuing further research in the United States. I must acknowledge that, for a lecturer, my trajectory was rather atypical. Indeed, I never enrolled in

a preparatory class or in any of the elite French universities, and I never sat for the exams that would confer
the highest teaching diploma in France. These are three
educational paths that normally would lead to the most
desirable and respected professorial posts in French higher
education.

Studying in France

Awarded a position within the French university system,
and frequently invited overseas, my scholarly trajectory
nevertheless began rather poorly. At the outset, nothing
would have seemed to point toward me being admitted
into the hallowed halls of the production and dissemi-
nation of French knowledge. In effect, though I had my
baccalaureate degree in hand, I was not assigned to the
university I had envisioned. My grades in English, my
favorite subject, had been excellent that school year, both
in the baccalaureate's written and oral portions. So I had
every hope of easily enrolling in the Parisian university of
my choice. I had often heard of the quality and the prestige
of the English department I had set my sights on, "one
of the best in France." But I had not taken into account
the administrative and socioeconomic dimensions of my
profile. Because, that is, I had graduated from a high school
in the suburban region of Paris, or *banlieue*, I was steered
automatically in the direction of my local university. It
was a simple matter of administrative logic. This logic
was entirely blind to geographic reality, inasmuch as to
get to that university would require a good hour on public
transportation (several buses, then the subway, or entirely
on the subway but for a longer commuting time), whereas
the Parisian university where I had so hoped to matriculate
was only a few subway stops away from where I lived.
I did my best to contest this assignment, which I found
completely arbitrary, with the Academy of Paris, but to

no avail. And so I found myself at the *banlieue* university for four years.

I am well aware that I am not alone in having experienced this disappointment. Nonetheless, what stands out in my memory to this day are the arguments presented to me by the various administrators I spoke with over the course of my efforts to challenge their decision. Among all of their arguments, the one that seems to me most revealing is the following: why did I persist in dreaming about this Parisian university when the education offered by each university was exactly the same? They continued to insist that the education offered by the university I wanted was no better than that offered by the one to which I had been assigned. The programs were more or less identical. They spoke of equal opportunity in education. I believed them. I resigned myself. Yet on obtaining my Master's degree, I could not help but be astonished by the fact that my research director at the time, who had been promoted to the faculty of a Parisian university, encouraged me to continue my studies with her in her new institution. According to her, this institution offered far better instruction and would prepare me for the *agrégation*, the most prestigious teaching diploma in France. I had no idea that my current university had no such preparatory program, nor was I aware that offering this preparation for the teaching exam constituted one of the markers of the quality and prestige of any given university. Four years prior, I had been told explicitly that all universities were the same. In reality, that was not the case at all.

And so I registered for classes in Paris. But in the course of that same year, I left for the United States as an exchange student. It was at that moment that everything was upended for me, both personally and intellectually. On the various campuses of the City University of New York (CUNY), I had access to courses on African history since the precolonial era and on Afro-Caribbean cultures,

I had seminars on Caribbean and African francophone literature and on the African diaspora. These courses amounted to a veritable feast. They inspired a real intellectual awakening, a genuine initiation. Over the course of that academic year spent in New York, I drafted a thesis on nineteenth-century Black nationalist thought in the United States and the imagination it created around Africa. With the credits I earned thanks to the courses and seminars I had taken during those two semesters, the thesis I wrote under the supervision of one of my New York professors was supposed to have been enough to earn me my French postgraduate diploma (MPhil).

It was only on returning to my Parisian university that my situation went downhill. I received all the necessary credits for the courses and seminars I had taken. Yet my thesis was not accepted. There were several reasons for this, according to my French research director. Some of these reasons had to do with substance. First of all, the very premise of my work had to be entirely revised. In effect, the notion of Black nationalism did not exist. Yes, I could work on the idea of nationalism, if I so desired. But no, that notion was not applicable to the populations I was working on – to African-Americans, that is. I had no idea what argument I could possibly make in response to that assertion, for I had spent the preceding academic year reading dozens of works and scholarly articles that were concerned specifically with the question of Black nationalism. The term was prevalent as much in the titles as in the content of works I had been consulting for months.

Since the end of the eighteenth century, Black nationalist thought in the Americas has developed an intellectual, political, and religious tradition that privileges a heightened idea of a Black and African identity. Black nationalism calls for racial separatism. Black nationalism also calls for emigration. Its basic premise is that the rise of racial democracy in American societies born of the modern era is impossible. Given this, the only possible solution is simply to leave those societies that are fundamentally hostile to Black peoples of the transatlantic diaspora for other, more welcoming and more egalitarian places. According to these notions, true acceptance or equality can only be found in Black countries, be they in the Americas (Haiti) or in the sub-Saharan African continent (Liberia or Ethiopia). According to Black nationalist thought, categorization based on racial belonging would replace categorization based on national belonging. In the context of the Black Americas, this nationalism existed in a variety of forms, including the back-to-Africa projects of the early nineteenth century, and various Pan-Africanist[2] currents, cultural nationalisms, and religious expressions. Some consider this to be a radical, if not extremist tradition. For me, it was precisely this radicalism that was interesting and that I wanted to explore intellectually. My fascination centered on the development of a certain imagination around the African continent and the memory thereof, as expressed by diasporic peoples born of the transatlantic slave trade. The question of origins, of home, and of return particularly interested me for the intimate, personal reasons I noted in the preceding chapter. These questions are central to Afro-diasporic studies, insofar as they enable detection and analysis of the systemic and systematic hostility of the host societies in which every diasporic population exists.

I was also reproached for the racist nature of my work. It was clear to my research director that I was not aware of the racism that so patently colored my project. I had to get a hold of myself. I absolutely had to avoid ruining the incredible potential that lay within me. The situation was not catastrophic: essentially, I had let myself get caught up in American "communitarianism." Now that I was back in Paris and in my enlightened and enlightening university, things would fall back into place.

I found myself completely dumbstruck in the face of this assessment of the work I had conducted for the past year.

I could accept a discussion of my methodology. I could also agree to discuss the terminology I had used, had it been possible to show me the linguistic invalidity of the term "Black nationalism." Yet, I *felt* that that is not what it was about. Without being able to put my finger on it, I wondered about the racist nature of the accusation that had just been made against me. Indeed, what meaning lurked within this accusation of racism in a color-blind country where the word race is itself taboo and where acts of racism are so rarely recognized and punished as such? In France, at the dawn of the twenty-first century, how could it be that this racism, a juridical rarity, was coming from *me*? A white-presenting woman was accusing me, a young Black woman, of racism. What did that mean? What exactly was the problem?

My use of the term *"nationalisme noir"* was nothing but a literal translation. So the problem could not be linguistic in nature. It is true that, in the interest of scholarly rigor, one might reasonably critique the use of the term to designate the political and religious tradition that had emerged from the Black Americas. In this case, it would suffice to replace it with a different term, one that would seem more adequate but that would designate the exact same phenomenon. So the problem was not one of nomenclature. What was, back then, merely an intuition led me to believe that my body and my phenotype were being brought into the discussion I was having with my research director. But this specific dimension of the discussion was latent, silent, perhaps even subconscious. In any case, it was not being clearly expressed. This being said, again, I *felt* that my Black identity had come into play. Even if my origins hark back to the African continent and not to the Americas, I seemed to share something with the populations that constituted my object of study. We had a body, a skin color in common. Why not, then, study this transnational racial identity? In other words, explore that which, historically, does and does not connect these populations? Yes, I was also, but not solely, interested in the Black Americas because I myself was Black. Beyond the identity question, there were intellectual, even philosophical, questions linked to the category of "Black," as well as the immense expanse of reflections that had been raised for centuries around these topics that I found equally interesting. Yes, I knew I was distinctly different from the Black Americans I wanted to study. There was a historical, not a personal, link between them and me. For I was well aware of the fact that Black Americans in general, and from the United States in particular, possessed a celebrated Black identity in France. Unlike Africans, these Black Americans were never perceived or presented as barbarous peoples to be civilized. The modern era, despite its totalizing and global violence, had granted them the status of civilizable and civilized. Thus, the Black African and Black US-American identity are not one and the same. Although both are anchored in complex and specific processes of historical racialization, they do not evoke the same imaginary. Nor do they evoke the same stereotypes. In the case of African-Americans (and this may seem paradoxical in light of the treatment they have received in the nation to which they belong), they find themselves associated with the positive and valorizing perception that France and Western Europe have of the United States. Seen from foreign spaces, the nationality of Black Americans underpins their racial categorization. They benefit from the powerfulness of their country. But no, apparently such considerations were inconceivable. Despite my African, Ivorian, Jula heritage, I was becoming a Black woman who studies Black people. I was a Black woman who identified with other Black people. Radical. A Black woman who could not possibly maintain critical distance from those Black people. A Black woman who wanted to resemble those Black nationalists of the nineteenth century. It was as if there was a danger that needed to be contained. A Black identity that needed to be policed. Politely, of course. And with great delicacy. Diplomatically. It would suffice to brandish the weapon of intellectual and scientific legitimacy: my research subject had no scholarly value.

On reading that episode from my life as a young researcher, some might accuse me of "assuming the worst" about my interlocutor at the time. But those sorts of arguments would be at once too easy and too practical. The major difficulty commonly faced by those who have experienced a racist, sexist, or sexual attack is the too-frequent impossibility of providing tangible, material evidence. But the scene I have just described makes sense to the extent that it happened within the institutional space that is the university. And so it is necessary to discern the power relations that play out there, against a backdrop of hierarchical associations that are articulated through age, social class, and university status. Race is then added to these elements. Because bodies do speak, despite the silence imposed by society. The body's words are the fruit of the history of France and many other Western powers in the modern era. This conversation, secret because silent, happens every day and everywhere – even and above all within institutions that are unable to imagine themselves outside of either the legacies of history or contemporary realities. Racism functions notably thanks to silence. This silence is imposed and maintained. Nonetheless, it rages on. It rages on all the more because it can be neither proven nor shown irrefutably. Indeed, it is rarely even spoken of aloud in France. Yet – and this is crucial – it is *felt*. Every time. When one experiences it, it is about a *feeling*: a gaze intercepted, heart palpitations, a sudden drenching in sweat, the feelings of injustice, anger, and frustration. But all of it is almost systematically relegated to silence. You didn't hear anything. Nothing was actually said. So nothing happened. The experience is denied you, confiscated. Yet, it is real. How then, can its existence be acknowledged? How can it be rendered audible and visible?

I was obliged to accept the rejection of my predoctoral thesis and to plan on redoing that academic year. I had to find a new research subject. This did not take too much time, as I was able to choose a new topic based on the year's-worth of work I had done in New York. I felt I had worked enough on the question of nationalism as related to the African continent, whether or not my thesis had been accepted. At this point, I wanted to work on the conditions that had led to the emergence of the Nation of Islam and the Rastafari movement from a diasporic perspective. It would be a matter of exploring the religious dimensions of Black nationalism. I was interested in the color of God, associated by these two groups with the true color of power. Such a project implicated the simultaneous study of two geographic regions: the United States and Jamaica. How my research director reacted when I announced my new project to her! ... This time, I really had to think. Of my career, of my future. Indeed, there is no such thing as a "Black Studies" department in France! What was I thinking? And besides, how did I plan to fund my doctoral studies? I would have to sign up for the teaching exams immediately! Since I already had a Master's degree, I had the great privilege of being able to sit for the *agrégation*!

In my eyes, the question of funding my studies had been part of my educational trajectory from the beginning, as I had always been on a scholarship, from primary school through university. Always at the maximum amount. Moreover, I had always taken on some professional activity in parallel with my secondary studies. So why would this question have any greater significance now? I was well aware that I had little chance of obtaining a doctoral fellowship. But that had no bearing on my capacities or my motivation, for I had grown up poor. I am talking about extreme precarity: large family, isolated single mother, neither running water nor telephone, reliant on the food bank, free medical coverage, unpaid bills, electricity cut off, foreclosures, vacations paid for by the Departmental Management of Health and Social Services[3] (never trips to the home country), Christmas gifts from the Red Cross, and housekeeping jobs during the school holidays. When it came to my university trajectory, this extreme precarity also meant not owning a computer, not having access to the Internet at home, and hoping with everything I had that the course textbooks would be available at the library.

Despite all of that, the family dream was one that is shared by so many poor or precarious immigrants: an unshakeable faith in social mobility through education. As such, despite everything, my household often seemed to be collapsing under the weight of books acquired at all costs; all the musical traditions of the world resounded there, and culture was sacred. The journey of migration, the gulf that grew ineluctably between France and our land of origin despite numerous and continuous efforts, the sacrifices and the low wages – it all had to be worth something, to have meaning. My relationship to prolonged higher education was, then, as follows: from a socioeconomic point of view, I had absolutely nothing to lose and everything to gain. My research director continued: why work on the Nation of Islam when that had been much studied already? Especially since Spike Lee's film on Malcolm X. As for the Rastas, surely I wasn't considering that! I would have to change my university course of study and enroll in Anthropology or Ethnology. None of this made any sense! My research director was beyond herself. She did not understand what could have happened to me during that year I had spent in New York. In less than a year, I had lost my mind. I who once had been so "clever," what a waste!

I, on the other hand, understood perfectly well what had happened to me over the course of that year. The experience had been extremely positive in my eyes.

I had finally become Black.

Of my own volition.

In France, I had grown up both Black and African. I became aware of these identities as a young girl. Many factors explain this. First of all, as I noted earlier, I grew up in a household where origins and detailed genealogy were of great importance and sources of great pride. Then, in the French Hexagonal space, I was constantly reminded of my alterity. In short, I did not fully belong to the true national community. I was a foreign body. Literally. As African-American sociologist W.E.B. Dubois so aptly described and theorized at the end of the nineteenth century with his concepts of the veil and of double consciousness,[4] my relationship with France was ambiguous, and France made me pay for that. I knew I was Black and African and that these two markers of my identity, which no one ever denied, did not fully have a place in the society in which I was being raised. These two markers of my identity, visible to the naked eye, had to be explained, justified, and diminished. I was supposed to not bother anyone, I was supposed to not take up too much space. I was meant to apologize for myself. Constantly. To apologize meant, especially, to not speak about identity. Or to agree not to speak about it other than within the frame of alterity and exteriority. Meaning that everything had to be considered through Africa or the Ivory Coast of my parents. There was no place for me. I did not exist. For in my case, if indeed I was of African, Ivorian, and Jula origin, I was no less Black and born in Paris, where I had grown up. What could I do with all of that? Until the 1990s and the consolidation of the independent French rap music scene, there had not been any word, any vocabulary, any discourse, or any space between my parents and France that could describe this experience – my experience: Black and French.

It was not possible to come to an agreement with that first research director on a new topic for my MPhil. So I decided to "run the risk" of abandoning my Parisian university for a provincial university. I was intent on obtaining the degree, for I planned on pursuing my doctoral studies. A new director was found. My research topic was no problem for her. All the better! But disillusion quickly caught up with me. In principle, I was effectively free to work on whatever I liked. However, I was expected to silently bear the at once recurring and loaded remarks concerning my origins, so legible on my body. This new thesis director boasted of helping African students. Was I one of them? If the response was yes, in what way? If the response was no, why mention it to me? What's more, during the period of the presidential election in France, she wondered why African women brought their children to political meetings. Something white women did not do, according to her. My new director also made me aware of what, in her eyes, I seemed to be giving off: radicalism. I will never know anything further on that front. No additional explanation was offered to me. But the deathblow was dealt when I was recruited to teach in one of the most prestigious universities in the United States: "Maboula, I'm not your mother, but I'm very proud of you. Congratulations! Let me give you a hug. It's clear you have the kind of profile that interests them. You're French, of course, but you know ... With your origins ... The Americans love that. It's the Rama Yade effect. Make the most of it!"

Ever since hearing these words spoken, I have had a peculiar relationship with Rama Yade, whom I do not actually know at all. At the moment when she emerged in the national political arena, she became a sort of archetype – a veritable symbol. Yade, as a young, Black, French woman bedecked with diplomas, seemed unique. She was the only one of her kind. A prototype. As a consequence, likely because at the same moment I was a doctoral candidate of visibly African origin, I cannot count the number of times I found myself compared to this woman politician. Yes, we were born in the same year, but not in the same countries. Yes, our respective families were Muslim. It was also the case that Rama Yade and I had both been raised in the Parisian *banlieue*, though with a vastly different level of social capital. And lastly, I simply had more degrees than Rama Yade. True, I had not matriculated at one of the prestigious universities, nor had I sat for and passed any exams as valued as the ones that dotted her path. Nonetheless, it seems important to note that, beyond the accreditation of directed research, there exists no State-authorized diploma higher than the doctorate. As such, I had difficulty grasping the meaning of these incessant comparisons with Rama Yade. Also, I refuse to bring up our diametrically opposed political sympathies or even the purely physical aspect of this improbable comparison: height, weight, facial features, style of makeup, hairstyle. All I know is that Rama Yade and I are two women. Two Black women. Rama Yade does not know it, but for several years and against my will, I was perceived as her doppelgänger.

A dozen years later, I became Sibeth Ndiaye.[5]

Studying overseas

It was in the United States that I defined myself as French and was accepted as such. No questions asked. No doubting my word. It happened very naturally. Almost automatically. Without the slightest effort. It was all quite simple: I found myself overseas and, very logically, I was often questioned about my origins. Each time, I responded that I came from France, from Paris. It was the first time that answer had come to me so easily. Up to that point, in France, my homeland, I had also been asked about my origins. Time and again. Each time, my response had been different: "I'm African," "I'm Ivorian." In truth, how I answered that question mattered little. It was enough for me to name a foreign country. A Black country. I had the feeling that, in a way, I did not really belong in France. I had to explain myself. To explain my presence. To explain the fact that I was Black. For it was neither my accent nor the way I dressed that inspired this questioning of my origins. It was my body, my phenotype, my hair, and maybe my first and last name. I did not belong. I came from somewhere else. I could not be French, I did not look French. I did not speak like a French person either. People would invent an accent for me – or else be astonished that I spoke French so well, that I did not have an accent. I did not eat like a French person. I did not pray like a French person either.

The United States and the distance that separated me from the Hexagon radically changed all of that. This new space, this third space (now added to the French Hexagon of my birth and the Ivory Coast of my parents) made me see Paris and the Hexagon as my homeland, my place of return. No one was more astonished than I. So astonished that when, in the first course I took on the Black/African diaspora taught by specialist Colin Palmer,[6] he casually announced that my hereditary African origins and my birth and residence in Europe meant that I, too, belonged to the very diaspora we students were about to study over the course of the semester, it was a genuine shock. A revelation. I had never seen things that way before. It suddenly became ridiculous, the way I would mock Erykah Badu and certain African-American artists in the rap or neo-soul music scene I so enjoyed. These artists' wardrobe choices had appeared to my ignorant eyes as having emerged directly from some exaggerated fantasy – that of a lost Africa rediscovered by means of reinvention. In reality, it was all just a matter of chronology.

I, too, had lost Africa.

However, I had long believed – wrongly – that my Africanness was unquestionable. I lived Africa and rubbed shoulders with it on a daily basis. Africa was my mother, my uncles and aunts, my family and Jula community. And I knew all too well how they all dressed. Their way of

dressing had very little in common with the outfits worn
by Badu and company, those rootless African-Americans
who invented and created for themselves a fluid and
illegitimate African identity. As for my Africanness, it was
truly legitimate because it was anchored.

I was wrong, but I did not yet realize it. I had not yet
acquired the tools to understand it. The reality was that
my own distance from the ancestral homeland was only
geographically and historically shorter. All that time,
I had firmly believed that my homeland was the Ivory
Coast, solidly planted in the African continent, and that
my destiny was to return there someday. As if I had to
choose between France and the Ivory Coast. As if I could
not hold on to both of them. And so it was that in the
United States, in New York, at the Graduate Center of the
City University of New York that a few words spoken by a
prominent Jamaican scholar, who happened to be making
his career there, shook up all my convictions about my
own identity. Up till then, I had believed that these convictions were mine. But in fact it was my parents who had
fabricated them. The republican discourse had also taken
part in constructing them. My center shifted. My personal
geography and chronology had been upended. Another
world opened up for me – a hybrid, fluid, diasporic
world. Édouard Glissant and Maryse Condé consolidated
this new world that was becoming mine. They added a
primordial touch to it: look at all the parts of France right
in the eyes. Look at the Hexagon and its relationship to
the world, to history, and to geography.

There is a great deal of scholarly work dedicated to
US-Black American migration to Europe in general and
to France in particular since the end of the nineteenth
century. In the case of migrations to France, studies have
been published by scholars from both the United States
and France. In both languages and in both countries, in
full-length monographs and in articles, Black identity,
race, and racism have been directly evoked, discussed,

commented on, and analyzed. It is often a question of the extraordinary and generally positive trajectories of African-Americans who found refuge in Paris and throughout the French Hexagon. Fleeing the absolute racism of US segregation, African-American soldiers, artists, intellectuals, and athletes found France to be a welcoming place that, in many instances, honored them and afforded them great success. The scholarly works that trace this story are legion. More difficult to find, on the other hand, are analyses that compare the treatment of African-American populations to that of other Black populations present in France during the same time periods. Is it that racial and racist constructions – that Black identity – only exists in the United States? Be it within the colonial or the postcolonial context, how can we explain this reticence – this inability – to recognize the ways in which racial categorization exists on French soil? France and the United States have a slaveholding and imperialist history in common. So why is it that scholars in France who have dedicated themselves to exploring matters of race in the United States are unable to do so in the place where they live and work?

In this regard, the enthusiasm generated in the university and media arena by Ta-Nehisi Coates's long stay in Paris in 2015 seems particularly revealing of that compartmentalized vision of the two sides of the Atlantic: can it be that, on the one hand, there is the United States, where race is widely deployed and, on the other, the French nation, where race has no meaning? Further, one of the other blind spots of scholarly research on Black American migration is that which concerns unfavorably racialized French people who leave France for the United States, where their experience of racism is, paradoxically, often minimized and where greater opportunity is possible. In the United States, as in Hexagonal France, there is much to be gained by not being native Black: such a status relieves the national and individual conscience and guarantees better social treatment. Of my own long experience in the United States, I well recall the extent to which I benefited from my Black French status. Although it was common for Americans to first see me as Haitian, due to my physical appearance and the fact that I spoke French, in the end, I was more often associated with the prestige of French culture and refinement. On many occasions, France's radiant image overseas, which it has made a point to amplify, played in my favor. I became a very useful Black woman, in that I did not incarnate the past of slavery and segregation in the United States. I was situated outside of the original racial conflict. This positioning alleviated tension. It is worth noting, however, that this position was only viable once I spoke. If silent, the situation was radically different, for in that case only my body and my way of dressing were audible. In that case, there was nothing to distinguish me from any other Black American – with all that meant in terms of othering and unfavorable treatment. The situation is no different for African-Americans settled in France: they are not part of the French problem. And by the same token, they enjoy the social benefits of this situation.

Each country has its own "Black."

I spent nearly ten years in the United States. Off and on. Primarily in New York, a singular city vis-à-vis the rest of the country. I spent ten years navigating the waters of the Atlantic Triangle, from one coast to the other, to the extent my meager financial resources allowed, based on whatever university or professional opportunities presented themselves, and on whether it was possible to obtain the required visas. As far as the latter was concerned, being a French passport-holder put me in a far better position than possessing an Ivorian one would have done. The unfettered circulation of people only applies to a portion of the planet's inhabitants: there is no equality when it comes to border policy. That being said, despite my theoretical privilege as a French woman, the authenticity of my French nationality proved itself somewhat fragile in many instances. It could be interrogated, examined, or called into question based entirely on the color of my skin and on my first and last names.

What did I learn from that long time spent in the US? I learned, first and foremost, that New York is a world-in-a-city made up of the diverse populations that live there. Demographic diversity is a simple fact there. To be clear, social, racial, and religious tensions can be extreme. However, the challenge posed by "the city that never sleeps" concerns the daily management of the diverse population. In New York, it has long been clear that the vast majority of immigrants who arrive there never leave. So it means making do with that fact. In this, New York is a deafening city, both literally and figuratively: it allows no space for silence.

In New York, I attended both public and private universities. I discovered departments dedicated to the following fields: Black Studies, African-American Studies, Pan-African Studies, Africana Studies, Women's Studies, and Ethnic Studies. These departments were not rarities – on the contrary. For the most part, they had emerged from the mobilization of students, who had played a major role in the civil rights movement. In effect, the socio-racial demands of the time had not overlooked the matter of education. As such, students had occupied campuses to demand that university leadership create new curricula and fields of study – to insist that these take minority groups into account and that they be integrated into traditional programs of study. It was a matter of expanding the vision of education by diversifying the canon. Moreover, these new programs had to be degree-granting and lead to concrete professional possibilities. Lastly, the creation of new programs of study automatically implied the recruitment of a new sort of professor. These new recruits had to be qualified members of minority groups. As such, these deep transformations of the higher education system were meant to happen both through the programs and through the literal bodies of the faculty.

When I spent my first academic year at the City University of New York, I had never had access to such a vast offering of courses. I had never been exposed to such vast diversity among my professors. This was a shock. The good kind. Professors who specialized in the African diaspora were thrilled to meet a "Soumahoro" in the flesh and encouraged me to look into researching my own ancestry. When it came to my family name, I no longer had to spell or pronounce it over and over again, as so often happened in France. They pointed out my illustrious heritage – real or imagined. And these words were not coming from the family lore so stubbornly maintained by my mother, but from perfect strangers in whom I found unbiased legitimacy. I could become an object of study – not because I was their "precious child," but historically. I read about Afro-diasporic cultures of the Americas for the first time: marronnage, candomblé, Vodou, santería, carnival. I discovered Caribbean and African theory. I learned about Africa and its history, finally discovering precolonial history: Mali, Songhai, Ghana, Kanem-Bornou. I read Deleuze and Guattari; I read about the African diaspora; I discovered Mudimbe, Hall, and Gilroy; I became interested in francophone literature of the Caribbean and Africa. It was all new. Another world opened up for me – a world to which I was free to belong. A world to which I had decided to belong.

New York and the United States were also spaces of opportunity: my first colloquia, my first presentation of a paper, my first teaching experience. New York also had museums, as well as public, private, and university libraries whose offerings devoted to the themes that interested me and that I was working on were far greater than those available to me in Hexagonal France. And as far as my research was concerned, I was never accused of racism in the United States. I was consistently encouraged there. The doctoral project I had begun was systematically considered innovative, precisely because I was comparing two distinct spaces of the Black Americas. Yes, the notion of diaspora, applied to peoples of near or distant African heritage spread throughout the Americas as a result of the trans-atlantic slave trade and the institutionalization of slavery, made complete sense. Moreover, this notion rightfully questioned and defied the nation-state model that, with its strict geographic frontiers, made little methodological sense in the study of Black American cultures. Why this vast disconnect between France and the United States?

When I say that I finally became Black of my own free will in the United States, I mean that it was there that I was instilled with a certain racial pride. Because it was there that I met individuals and communities that had no need to hide themselves in order to exist. Communities that, after so many struggles, had gained access to spaces, degrees, and roles that had no equivalent in France. In these spaces, in these roles, Black identity neither disap-peared nor dissolved. Nor did it seem to apologize for itself. It was on the basis of this uncomplicated Black identity that all of this richness was built – something, that is, that could be recognized as valuable to outsiders. Something, at least, that could be expressed publicly – that was not confined to the private sphere. In this respect, it was the exact opposite of the French situation. For in the context of the United States I became aware that I had, in fact, made a detour. This distance I had taken with respect to Africa, to the Ivory Coast of my parents, and to my home in the Hexagon, had made me lose sight of my own identity as a Black woman. I was not *either* African, Ivorian, Jula, or French. Becoming Black was a matter of political solidarity, of a transnational cultural and intel-lectual connection. I was rooted in this Atlantic space. Historically. But I had also made that determination. This detour to the United States revealed to me both the invisibility of my French experience and my ambivalence with respect to my parents' home country. The distance allowed me to return to myself. Studying Black Americans was now pushing me to do so with Black French people. It had not been possible to do so before. The detour had proven necessary, fundamental. It had been a matter of distancing myself in order to return. It had been a matter of distancing myself in order to return under better circumstances – by putting an end to all that had been silenced, or unconsidered when it came to race. After ten years, my return to my homeland was complicated. I was leaving a space where race was visible – hyper-visible, even – for one that was exceptionally blind to the matter.

3

The Hexagon

An Ambiguous Adventure

"He had thought again about their nervous adolescent shapes pacing up and down the neighborhood so long ago – how prepared they had been to connect lovingly with France. But there had been no love; they had arrived in the middle of a forty-year war, which was ongoing. And so at the end of the hymn, when the words 'impure blood' were sung, they had lowered their heads and raised their fists. John Carlos, French remix, fuck it all."

– Jean-Éric Boulin, *Nous aurons de l'or*
[We Will Get the Gold] (2014)

The preceding chapters are merely pretexts. For, in reality, they have all led to the subject that so urgently and so perennially interests us. The subject at hand is the Hexagon – this birthplace, this place I call home. This ambiguous country. It is in this space that contemporary problems and tensions that touch and concern us here are playing out and unfolding. Whether we like or not. Moreover, I notice that my reflections cover two decades: 1999–2019. The first decade was spent primarily in New York, while it is in Paris that I spent the latter.

"For the great MCs, on behalf of a grateful 'hood'"[1]

In 1999, I believed that the jacket cover for the rap group Ideal J's album *Le combat continue* [The Fight Continues] would be enough to garner me a teaching post in French at Wesleyan University in the United States. I did not get the job. I had come in second, and the final decision had been very close. The interview had gone extremely well. Two American professors, sent to Paris by their university in order to conclude this recruitment process, had listened attentively to me. Then 23 years old, I had decided to give them a different picture of France. One that was neither the best known nor the most boasted about on the other side of the Atlantic. Nevertheless, this was the France I claimed. It was the France of rap, the France of the Parisian *banlieue*, the France of the Parisian outskirts. A Black France. To illustrate this, what better than the jacket of that mythical album that revealed, against a black background, a Black man's hand gripping the French flag?[2] The tension in the image was palpable, evident: the Black male hand and the French flag almost seemed linked, inseparable. Then, on the back of the jacket of this vinyl record, there was a second image of equally important symbolic value: the body of a Black man draped in the tricolor flag, assuming the pose of Marianne, the French Lady Liberty. Rich, powerful, eloquent images that amounted to a pedagogical gold mine. Moreover, it was a matter of *my* France, the one I came from, the one that knew me, recognized me, and said something about who I am. It would, I thought, attract the attention – and arouse the interest – of American students, students who were also filled with questions about race and identity in their country and whose contemporary and historical reality clearly had proven to be no melting pot. They listened to me attentively. They believed me. They expressed great interest in my rather unexpected approach. The final decision was close. Wesleyan was not to be. But there was still the City University of New York.

French rap, as an artistic offering endowed with its own innovative aesthetic, counts among the few spaces of postcolonial France where questions linked to immigration, identity, dual culture, race, and the idea of the multiple homes one can claim can be addressed without hesitation. In 1994, the group Ministère A.M.E.R. released its most accomplished album, for which it chose the title of the zip code shared by the majority of the group's members: 95200.[3] In addressing a "personal message" to all "Negros," as well as declaring the year 1994 "white and dry,"[4] these rappers from Sarcelles, a Parisian *banlieue*, rooted their Black, African, and Antillean identity in the Hexagon. Throughout the entire album, the group of rappers laid claim to and mapped out the Hexagon, extracting their cultural and political references from it with humor and derision. Three years later, with the track "Blessé dans mon ego" [My Wounded Ego], Ekoué, member of the collective La Rumeur [The Rumor],[5] expounded on the problems linked to "his African epidermis," his double French and Togolese culture, to colonial and postcolonial French history – problems that play out on intimate, familial, and political levels. The track also asks the question of how to find or to fashion a home between Togo, land of his parents; Hexagonal France, his birthplace and current residence; and the United States and the hip-hop culture he – along with so many others of his generation – claimed as his own.

This is the same relationship to Hexagonal France, to his parents, and to the land of his origins that the rapper Rim'K from the group 113 explores in his song "Tonton du bled" [Uncle from Back Home], which came out in 1999. This rapper from the *banlieue* offers a detailed description of a simple summer holiday back in the hometown of a young French Algerian man. Just like the Togolese homeland of the rapper Ekoué, the Algerian homeland evoked by Rim'K immediately harks back to French colonial history. Racial categorization – be it a function of the body, of phenotype, or of religion – was the currency. The track "Tonton du bled" once again reveals the intergenerational tensions born of the inevitable gap carved out between the expectations of immigrant parents and those of children born or raised in the Hexagon. The track is peppered with words in Arabic, the rapper's native language. These words are mixed in with French, slang, and *verlan*[6] as well. And whereas at the end of the track Rim'K declares his desire to end his days "over there, Inch'Allah," it is nonetheless a return "to the projects" that ends the story and that has been expected all along. One cannot help but be struck by the way the return to the projects seems concrete, while the sacred wish to end his days in Algeria so as to respect his parents' wishes seems to be belied by the "Inch'Allah." Moreover, the chorus of the track marks a clear opposition between the paternal injunctions and the son's attempted negotiation:

> I wanted to stay in the projects, my father told me, lā lā lā
> In that case I'll bring along all my friends, lā lā lā
> So in a week I'll go back to Vitry, lā lā lā
> I'll go finish my days over there, wah wah wah.

Although approached with humor, this one-on-one encounter unfolds bluntly through the multiple "nos" (lā) and the sole "yes" (wah) pronounced by the father. The son "wanted to stay in the projects" or to leave on the condition that he can "bring along" all his friends, and only stay in Algeria for a week. The visit ends up lasting a month. And although one can feel the rapper's respect for his parents' homeland, his real home remains Vitry-sur-Seine, a region of the Parisian *banlieue*. In the track by Rim'K of 113, the deliberate use of the Arab language combined with the sample from the classic song "Harguetni Eddamaa," sung by the great Algerian singer Ahmed Wahby, emphasizes the nonwhite dimension of the identity he claims and to which he so proudly pays homage. This identity is nonetheless rooted in the Hexagon: the periphery of Paris. This identity is also hybrid: inherited from his parents, it is nonetheless remixed – hip-hop style – by DJ Mehdi. In this sense, the parental culture does not amount to a legacy handed down directly, without contestation. Hip-hop allows him to claim and transform that non-French parental culture, to let it be simultaneously contested, negotiated, and refashioned by that son of immigrants raised in France, where he is confronted by his own reality and his Frenchness. The fact of freeing himself from parental constraints and culture or of rebelling against them is by no means about rejecting them. It can also be a question of repositioning himself in the light of his own experience.

Lastly, in 2006, another rap song once again brought up the question of home. With "Chez moi" [At Home], Casey[7] lays claim to Martinique, land of her parents' birth. She evokes several essential cultural figures: "Frantz Fanon, Aimé Césaire, Eugène Mona, and Ti Émile," as well as "kinky hair," "big lips," and "mix of melanin." In doing so, she shifts the focus toward one of the current so-called overseas territories, while situated in the Hexagon. Let us also note that "Chez moi" was released at a time when the realization and diffusion of video clips had become commonplace and presented a visual aesthetic specific to rap.[8] Therefore, the tracks present an additional level of meaning: the image that serves to illustrate – to illuminate, even – a particular aspect of the lyrics. That is, the video directed by Chris Macari highlights a fundamental aspect of Casey's track: its transatlantic nature. In effect, the title "Chez moi" offers a direct parental vision of the genealogical link that connects Casey to the island her parents and her ancestors came from. Macari's video amplifies

the original musical narrative with the help of images –
making the decision to film "Madinina, island of flowers"
as extensively as he films images of the Parisian *banlieue*
or the city of Paris. What emerges from this visual layout
is the link and the connection between the places in
question: the so-called overseas country, Martinique, and
Hexagonal France. And that France includes both Paris
as a symbol of the center and the *banlieue* that makes up
the periphery. What becomes clear is the impossibility of
talking about Martinique without evoking the Hexagon.
For Martinique is aware of the Hexagon, while the inverse
is not true. Yet these two spaces make up Casey's home;
the space of Martinique exists. From the status of colony,
it acquired that of "overseas department" in 1946.

Several years later, the production team of a French
television station that had hoped to show more "diversity"
on screen, ultimately abandoned the idea of having me
as a guest, under the pretext that a university lecturer
– an intellectual – would not be capable of having a
discussion with a rapper, even one well known to the
wider public. That she would not be capable of engaging
in conversation with a rapper on equal intellectual
footing. As if rappers had never produced or expressed
any ideas. And all this without being able to imagine
that in fact I personally knew the rapper in question.
Indeed, we came from the same neighborhood and had
hung out together since we were kids, notably because
of the importance that hip-hop had in both our lives.
Nonetheless, my trajectory seemed unimaginable: if it was
possible to envisage the connection rapper–disadvantaged
neighborhood, it was, on the contrary, impossible to
make the connection university professor–disadvantaged
neighborhood. My social status at the time thus erased
my very modest origins in the *banlieue*. However, rap
and hip-hop culture largely contributed to my intellectual
development.

2005: "Right the wrong, by any means necessary"[9]

I spent ten years moving between Paris and New York. By chance, I found myself in France in October and November 2005, when the uprisings that took place in the wake of the deaths of Bouna Traoré and Zyed Benna and the serious injury of Muhittin Altun occurred. The uprisings unfolded in popular neighborhoods throughout the Hexagon, due to the mass media coverage and to the sustained political and institutional interest these tragic events generated. It was in the course of these events that, in this secular land, political figures publicly led an absurd and completely useless fatwa against the "rioters." It was in the course of these events that rappers were deemed the true culprits in the uprisings. Yet these rappers had not in fact encouraged them. Rather, they had announced, understood, and described them, as is evidenced in songs like Ministère A.M.E.R.'s "Sacrifice de poulets" [Chicken Sacrifice][10] and "Qu'est-ce qu'on attend" [What Are We Waiting For] by NTM,[11] which had come out ten years prior. It was also during the course of these events that it became preferable to deem those they called "the rioters" foreigners whose papers could be taken away and who could be deported *manu militari* if they were caught red-handed. It was essentially impossible to see these young troublemakers, these ghetto youth, these residents of lower-class neighborhoods as true French citizens. Which was most often who they were.

It was in such a context that I wrote my first article about France.[12] Following some fieldwork carried out with an African-American colleague, Trica Keaton, in the Clichy-sous-Bois neighborhood, the article was published in an American journal. It considered the events of fall 2005 and, based on lyrics taken from rap productions since the 1990s, offered an analysis of the counter-discourse that encompassed the totality of the problems that had emerged in the space of Hexagonal France and comprised the core of public discourse related to the *banlieue* circulating at the time in the media and various institutions: discourse around repression, national security, the role of the police, police brutality, the role of the schools, educational failure, unemployment, racism and discrimination, social exclusion, precarity, immigration, impossible assimilation, the limits of integration, Islam, cultural specificities, the weight of history, colonial amnesia. This being said, at the time I was struck mainly by the paradoxical nature of the situation. In effect, my African-American colleague Trica Keaton, who held a PhD in sociology, had carried out a portion of her university cursus at the School of Advanced Study in Social Science.[13] She had devoted her research to the race question in Hexagonal France, considered particularly through the prism of the *banlieue* and of Islam.[14] As I have already noted, my university training had been focused on Black identity in the United States and the Anglophone Americas. With the events of 2005, our two trajectories seemed to intersect and connect.

Up until then, Trica had been my object of study, given her belonging to the African-American community and, on my end, I had been hers. I ended up returning to a subject that it had been impossible for me to see or to be capable of considering before: myself and, more broadly, ourselves. That is, people from the *banlieue* – from working class or underprivileged backgrounds, and of direct or distant African heritage. Those who are infinitely recognizable, discriminatable, and stigmatizable due to their skin color, their clothing, their way of speaking or, even, of walking. It was a matter of homecoming. I was not from the same neighborhood as the three teenagers from Clichy-sous-Bois, nor was I from the same borough. Nonetheless, we shared a certain territorial familiarity, a similarity of life experience as poor people and as Black people. For anyone who knows even a little bit about West Africa, it is easy to understand how the name Bouna Traoré resonated with aspects of my own culture. In 2005, it became no longer possible for me to hide behind Black Americans to understand the functioning and consequences of racial categorization. It had become necessary for me to confront – to face up to – my own experience in my native land. Turning a blind eye had become impossible.

Beyond the events that shook up the Hexagon in October and November, the year 2005 was remarkable from the point of view of the numerous organizations, events, and publications that were launched into the public debate, which had reached the limits of its capacity for color-blindness. Among these were the passage of the historical memory law "acknowledging the Nation and the national contribution in favor of repatriated Frenchmen," whose Article 4, which placed an emphasis on the "positive role" of French colonization, was finally repealed a year later; the "declaration of the Indigenous of the Republic Party";[15] the creation of the Representative Council of Black Organizations in France;[16] the fires that destroyed several of the most inexpensive Paris hotels, known for sheltering primarily visibly foreign families; and, lastly, the foundational collective research publications, written in French, that made up *La Fracture coloniale* [The Colonial Divide][17] and *De la question sociale à la question raciale?* [From the Social Question to the Race Question?],[18] published just a year later. The race question, so far as it was playing out in the contemporary Hexagonal context, had become visible, audible, and a subject of scholarly inquiry. This same scholarly interest took a decisive turn three years later with the publication of *La Condition noire* [The Black Condition],[19] by the historian Pap Ndiaye. The race question had, quite simply, become inevitable. It had come to pose a challenge to republican universalism.

I also found myself in Hexagonal France at the outset of the 2007 presidential campaign and of the sharp turn right-wing political parties had decided to take at that moment. Public debate about national identity became a leading political issue. It even gave birth to the Ministry of Immigration, Integration, National Identity, and Co-development – as well as to a major national debate around these topics. All of this occurred in the wake of elections won and racism taken on in earnest. But it was not until the summer of 2009 that I returned to settle in France "for good." I had just obtained a job as Associate Professor. The time of my professional precarity had come to an end, finally. For a long time I had hesitated between the United States and my birthplace. In the end, preferring to play the professional stability card rather than follow my personal desire, I chose France. And so I took on my new role in September of that very year. Barely three months after my arrival in my new university, I had the pleasure of receiving the below email:

Hello, my dear Maboula.
After lowering myself to read your thesis, "What Color is God?," I could not hold back my disdain for your so very eloquent ideas. To begin with, the diaspora is not without connection to a key moment in history, and must not be used just any which way. In effect, this term is indissociable from the Jewish people.
    "I would also like to thank the professors and scholars who, over the years, have contributed greatly to my intellectual development" = apparently their efforts have failed mightily and, in your place, I would not be thanking them!!!
    This list cannot possibly be exhaustive "For your information, Maboula, the 'e' in the verb 'être' has a circumflex; to write a thesis that messes up the most basic rules of spelling, I have a hard time believing you're capable of teaching in a university!
    God must regret having made you Black only to one day read such a deplorable tale of Africa.

You're perfectly content in this thesis to spew ideas that have already been proven – you offer no new explanation. Your thesis is nothing more than warmed up old ideas

A three hundred page-long thesis, each page duller than the next. Why take three hundred pages to say something no one will ever want to read? Why didn't you choose a different topic? less centered on yourself…

Very sincerely yours,

Philippe Le Gaillou [*sic*]

Although the message was signed "Philippe Le Gaillou," the name associated with the email address was "Mamadou Tarah." I will never know the real identity of the person who sent me this message. Having done some digital sleuthing, I can affirm only that the message was sent from the university in which I was teaching. Though the university is spread out over multiple sites, I know also that the message came from my own campus. Moreover, the person who sent me the message knew that I had just returned from the United States and that I had been teaching there. Indeed, the message showed up in my Barnard College inbox. The anonymous writer seemed well informed, for it would have made more sense to write to me at Columbia University, which was more well known in France. Or perhaps it sufficed to know that Barnard College is part of Columbia University? Whatever the case, I never thought the message had been written by one of my students. The author of the message seemed perfectly aware of my recent doctoral defense, which had taken place in that very university just over one year earlier. From the outset, the author of the message questioned my legitimacy as a teacher. Only three months after I had taken on the role.

Later, I continued to receive similar messages more regularly, to my personal email or on social media, all questioning and denouncing my right to teach or to appear in the media. Each time, it was a question of my supposed lack of qualifications or competency, the color of my skin, my non-French origins, and my religion. As concerns the latter point, I should note that one day I received, at my home address, an explicitly Islamophobic anonymous letter.

Determined to file a criminal complaint with the police, I found myself faced with decided reticence from the officer who received me that day. Indeed, this represent-ative of the forces of law and order had trouble grasping the substance of my claim since the anonymous letter I presented to her mentioned Islam and Muslims. As far as she could tell, I did not resemble what she believed a Muslim should look like. What was visible to the naked eye – what she was able to see clearly – was that I was Black. So I had to muster all my patience and, above all, show great determination. It was essential that I be aware of and confident in the social privileges I now benefited from so that this complaint would be registered. For we are not all equal in the face of these institutions. In this secular country, in this republican institution, I had to declare myself Muslim and, therefore, a specific target of the sentiments contained in the anonymous letter that had been sent to my domicile. The author of the letter was likely trying to impress upon me the fact that they were well aware of my home address. Unlike the national police, this individual had no doubt as to my Muslim identity. Perhaps I should applaud that individual's more realistic vision, as well as their acceptance of the fact that one can be at once Black and Muslim? Much later, a family member – who still lived in the district where I grew up, but had not lived there for a long while – received an anonymous letter from someone seeking to express their displeasure with ideas I had shared on television the evening prior. On each occasion, I was being told to be quiet, to go back "to my country"; and the fact that my salary as a civil servant in the higher education system is paid by French taxpayers was decried.

I, *too*, am France.

Public discourse

What, then, does one have the right to say in the public sphere? Who has access to a public platform in this country that belongs to us all? What are the conditions of such access? My experience of the French media (television and radio) since 2012 has taught me the following. I am fully aware of the stakes of representations that are implicated in my appearances on television. In the course of these interventions, I am also aware of the staging of the programs and debates to which I am invited. I know the role I am meant to play. But I also know the role I have decided to play based on my own agency. First of all, as a woman, several attributes must be taken into account: my age, the color of my skin, my hairstyle, my weight. Then, too, it is important to take the tenor of my comments into consideration. Finally, it is a matter of putting these two sets of data into relation. For it is of course the relationship between each of these categories that allows me to illustrate my point. So it is that a well-respected and even more mediatized intellectual can call the management of Radio France to complain about the nonsense being spilled by "some African" featured on the air. Thus has it happened that, on television, someone thought they were complimenting me by describing me as "astonishing" because of how "articulate" I am. An older man, known to be quite cultivated and socially privileged, who describes himself as "heterosexual, native French, white, and Catholic," declares "I cannot stand seeing mosques in France," and is perfectly comfortable doing so. There is no outcry. It is not a matter of there being different standards for different perspectives, but rather of different standards for different bodies.

On another television show, during the taping of the program, I once engaged in a heated debate with a secondary school teacher, author of several books, most of which concerned the social problems plaguing contemporary Hexagonal France. It is readily apparent that the point of departure for her work is complete annoyance with anyone who seriously studies French society as it is in reality rather than the fantasy. The author is a media figure who enjoys some measure of prestige. That is to say, she is frequently invited to promote her publications. She has easy access to participation in public discourse. Let us keep in mind that this is a rare and precious thing, which is the equivalent of saying that public discourse and access thereto is eminently political. In the course of this debate, which was fierce, this secondary school teacher suddenly spat out – completely veering away from the topic at hand – "Publish your thesis!" That sentence has haunted me ever since. In that moment, I was astounded. I only managed to answer something along the lines of: "Even if you don't bother writing a thesis, it seems you still can be a guest on TV – so don't worry." But her demand haunted me long after we finished taping that show. I will now try to analyze it and to discern its deeper meaning.

To my eyes, "Publish your thesis!" is revealing of a certain discomfort, of bad faith, of an inability to accept my social status in light of my racial identity. I see this demand as a desperate attempt to disqualify my intellectual legitimacy. For it is important to remember that access to public discourse is based on the matter of legitimacy, of whatever nature. As such, in the context of a television show devoted to the discussion of ideas, the titles and statuses of the guests are what matter. If this woman and I are invited to these sorts of shows, those invitations are determined on the basis of our respective titles: she, as a high school teacher and the author of an essay; me as a professor and scholar with a position in a university. Our respective statuses validate our legitimacy. As such, it is on this basis that I believe "Publish your thesis!" and the indisputable imperative it contains deserve particular attention, given the great symbolic violence they reveal.

In effect, it was not a matter of designating me by my title, foundation of my legitimacy, but rather of pointedly undermining my title. As such, because my status as a PhD holder is undeniable, it became about emphasizing a supposed deficiency in this status, as I had not published my doctoral thesis.[20] Which would make me, in the end, a false scholar. A false intellectual. An impostor. This status is reinforced by my physical appearance. I do not have the right color for a scholar. In fact, I do not have the right color for an intellectual. The lie thus becomes easier to believe or, in any case, to be well received by those ready to hear the kind of rhetoric that targets certain bodies. It should be noted that the university does not oblige publication of the doctoral thesis after receiving the diploma. But above all, this call to order – this evocation of false rules, rules that supposedly govern the functioning of the university – was coming from a high school teacher. A teacher who held no doctorate. A teacher who was not an Associate Professor and had neither sat for nor passed a qualifying examination to obtain a position in a public institution of higher education.

What I am interested in bringing to light here is the lack of respect for social hierarchy. Yes, society is organized hierarchically and inequitably. In this context, from a social point of view, a university professor is superior to a high school teacher. A secondary school teacher should not then be in a position to demand, publicly and perfidiously, that a professor in higher education "publish her thesis." That should not make sense. It should have no power and should produce no effect. This high school teacher nonetheless knew exactly what purpose this false, albeit performative, utterance would serve. Whether consciously or unconsciously does not matter, as only the results are important in the end. This high school teacher deployed the sole weapon that remained at her disposal to right the social balance that otherwise worked against her. The sole weapon at her disposal to right the intellectual balance.

The sole weapon that could play in her favor – if we accept the principle according to which diplomas are the mark of intelligence and the justification of the right to legitimate public discourse – was the color of her skin. Her white skin, in this staged context that was the television studio, fundamentally imbued her with legitimacy and authority over my Black skin.

In the space of this highly formatted audiovisual scenario to which we had both subjected ourselves, who would bother to be concerned with the technical aspects of our respective titles? The white-presenting woman demanded that the Black-presenting woman "publish her thesis." Although it was a question of a doctoral thesis, the word "doctorate" was never spoken. It did not matter. No one heard it and no one needed to hear it. The white-presenting woman made the Black-presenting woman out to be an unrealized intellectual, an intellectual who had failed because she did not make it to the very end of the rigorous scholarly path. The Black-presenting woman thus was not an intellectual. Or not as much of an intellectual as the white-presenting woman. Who did not have a doctorate, but who is white – that is to say, more readily credible as a PhD holder or an intellectual. From the outset. This credibility, which more or less goes without saying, can be explained as much historically, as culturally, socially, economically, and statistically. I am familiar with and spend time with my French colleagues and cannot help but notice the color of their skin. Moreover, I can no longer keep track of the number of times my Black woman's body has been perceived as contradicting my title: I am rarely the lecturer that students, colleagues, or administrative personnel expect. In an effort to justify their surprise on meeting me, they often mention my "young" age or my clothing – they have even found it easier to think of me as foreign or Anglophone. Prior to meeting, given my first and last name, they might have thought I would be a man, and thus might be taken aback upon meeting the woman I actually am. By contrast, the color of my skin is never mentioned. Yet, I am not that young. I do not know how the clothes I wear might be subject to interpretation. And, although I am bilingual, I do not have the impression that I express myself in such perfect English as to be mistakeable for an Anglophone foreigner. In that regard, I should add that passing for an Anglophone foreigner can even happen when I speak to one or another of my colleagues in French. And of course it goes without saying that only a cisgendered[21] man can embody with any authority the knowledge associated with the role of university professor.

Aside from the particular example I brought up earlier, it has also been important to me to think about what had allowed – what had authorized – this woman to give me an order, in defiance of all social logic. You can say what you like. You can try to convince me with as many arguments as possible, but it will be impossible to convince me nonetheless. My conclusion is as follows: the white-presenting woman demanded that the Black-presenting woman stay in her place. The simple fact that I was socially superior to her had already challenged her vision of the natural order of things. That was intolerable. I should not have been – I could not be – above her. So what does it matter if it takes a show of bad faith when it comes to maintaining her supposedly legitimate status – when the stakes are the preservation of her privilege? The privilege of appearing white and getting all the usual benefits out of it, among which: reason, authority, legitimacy.

Another woman, also white-presenting, a PhD holder and Lecturer, was on set as well. She was not the one who ordered me to publish my thesis. In her eyes, we were equals and that did not seem to bother her; her issues with me were entirely different. The person for whom I posed a problem knew that I was socially superior to her. And it was the fact that this superiority was working in my favor in this case that seemed to pose a problem for

her. A problem that had to be rectified. At whatever cost.
Should I mention that this questioning of the legitimacy of
the guests did not extend to any of the men on the show?
We might, undoubtedly, discuss the limits of feminine or
feminist solidarity when the race question comes into play.
Or perhaps my Black identity cancels out my identity as
a woman?

All the Women Are White.

Intersectionality is not a myth.

My entry into the world of the media happened upon
my return from the United States. It was the very essence of
that country that attracted media interest in me at the time.
Since then, I know that I have to reactivate it regularly.
Otherwise the scent loses its effect and the invitations
become more infrequent. So from time to time, I return
to the United States. Always happily, of course. However,
I certainly recognize the somewhat obligatory nature of
this approach. In effect, what is emphasized most often
when I am introduced is my affiliation with American,
rather than French, institutions of higher education. But
that is not always the case. In effect, being affiliated with a
prestigious Parisian institute of higher learning also opens
doors. This is the case even if that prestigious school is
not the one where one has a permanent position, that is,
the place where one spends the majority of one's annual
working hours. Are not all institutions of higher learning
meant to be equal?

The first television program I participated in had specifically invited me to address a question related to the notions
of equivalence and equality I have just brought up here.
It was in 2012. A minister in the French Republic had
recently made a statement that was deemed sensationalist
by several media outlets and political figures. Controversy
ensued. Evoking "French civilization," the minister had
declared that not all civilizations had value, that some
were superior to others. The sentiments expressed by
this minister did not shock me at all. I found them

unsurprisingly widespread. By contrast, what I found more shocking was the reaction to these sentiments. More specifically, the avalanche of reactions. The astonishment and condemnation were nearly unanimous. This struck me for the simple reason that we were in 2012 and a fringe of the Hexagonal French population seemed to have just learned something new: the existence of a fundamentally inequitable, because hierarchical, vision and approach to the world, to civilizations, and to human beings. That could only be astonishing. Historically speaking. That said, what was even more surprising was the direction this controversy took when the Prime Minister and an elected official from one of the so-called overseas territories came onto the scene.[22] Called to task on the statements made by his minister, bitterly critiqued by the "overseas" official, the Prime Minister decided to leave the National Assembly along with his entire government. The insult to the government was deemed unacceptable: it had been compared to the Nazi regime. At least that was what the vast majority of the press focused on. However, in paying attention to the totality of the criticism made by the elected official, the unacceptable, "indecent" comparison was not limited to the Nazi regime alone.[23] It suffices to look a little closer at the Martinican elected official's full statement to realize that the argument he put forward was entirely Césairean:[24] "Day after day, you bring us back to those European ideologies that gave birth to the concentration camps, to the end of the long rosary of slavery and colonization."

In effect, Aimé Césaire, iconic Black man, has theorized the genealogy and multiple evolutions of Western violence. Product and accessory of the modern era, that violence was first deployed widely outside of Europe before returning to explode, perfectly logically, during World War II. That is, because Europe was at the origin of the violence, it was inevitable that it be contaminated by it – struck, sooner or later, at its very core. Invited to weigh in on the subject of this controversy on television, I limited myself to noting that the minister's statement was part of a broader school of thought: that of the West, which, historically, had spread throughout the world on the basis of the very logic he had evoked. Taking that into account, the Martinican official's reminder in the wake of the minister's statement made perfect sense. Who better than those who come from the so-called overseas territories to remind the Hexagon of the precise and concrete consequences of a hierarchical view of civilizations and peoples?

Black History Month (BHM)/Africana Days

It was ultimately in 2013 that the Black History Month Association was created, under my leadership. This is a cultural organization that situates itself in a transatlantic perspective and aims to promote the history and culture of the Black world. Given that these topics are so rarely attended to in the French public sphere, it aims to make up for a general lack of information, knowledge, and acknowledgment. The organization attempts to organize annual events and to offer them at no cost. In fact, we make a point to avail ourselves of public funds so as to ensure they are free. In our eyes, this is an acceptable form of reparation for the long national history of racism, discrimination, exclusion, and marginalization at work in the fields of culture and education. This approach has led to several rather amusing moments in which, in discussion with partners who are in a position to offer us financial or logistical support, or to provide an event space, we find ourselves obliged to defend the interest, legitimacy, and peaceful nature of our activities. The greatest risk on this front is that of passing for a "communitarian" organization. This is a serious accusation with significant consequences: like the blocking of access to public spaces and withdrawal of financial support. It is an accusation that is never made against white-identifying people, even though "race doesn't exist."

Returning to the matter at hand, I should note that for one of the Africana Days events, organized in partnership with tRIBa Prod[25] around the topic of hybrid identity, one of the venues we had contacted and that had volunteered to host us was concerned about how we were planning to promote the event. The theme had been explained clearly, but the conversations that followed gave the impression that there had not been any initial discussion. Strangely, when it comes to certain topics, communication can get more difficult, nonsensical, even – unusually and disconcertingly irrational. As ideas for the visual promotion of the planned debates on the question of hybrid identity, we were offered a series of photos presenting: Senegalese colonial riflemen; Malcolm X; Martin Luther King; the Black Panthers; and Muhammad Ali fighting a cartoon character. In other words, it was suggested that we promote our event using images of Africans, African-Americans, and even a fictional character. I see this example as extremely telling in that it shows, once again, the difficulty for a certain sector of the Hexagonal French population to conjure up the existence or the presence of Black French people within the space of the Hexagon – as if a detour through the African or the American continent is always required. No rootedness in Europe seems to be imaginable. Never. Or else with great difficulty. With the exception of one person, all those who had agreed to participate in this annual Black History Month Africana Days event were French – with origins in Guadeloupe, Nigeria, Cambodia, Martinique, Brazil, Russia, the Comoros Islands, and North Africa. So we had to find a suitable promotional image ourselves.

One of our organizers came up with a brilliant idea. The idea was brilliant for two reasons. First of all, the idea she proposed succeeded in capturing the essence of what Black History Month and tRIBa Prod had in mind.

Second, the idea was legible to our speakers. It consisted of taking the cover of *Survival*, the album released by the indispensable Bob Marley and the Wailers,[26] as a point of departure. With its collage of African flags and sketch of a slave ship and its human cargo at their center, the album cover has clear Pan-African symbolism. For Black History Month and tRIBa Prod, it was a matter of replacing the flags from the Jamaican album cover with those of the ancestral homelands of our speakers, the members of the organization, as well as of those influences and sources of inspiration that mattered to the organization. Ultimately put together by our own efforts, the promotional poster included, among others, the independentist flags of Martinique and Guadeloupe, the national flags of Nigeria, the Comoros Islands, France, and the United States, as well as the African-American version of the latter, created by the artist David Hammons. What seems most important to pay attention to here is the fact that it was impossible for our partners to understand the imaginary that we wanted to highlight. In some respects, we were not speaking the same language. Despite the fact that we all shared the French language, it was a matter of undertaking a true effort of translation. It was impossible for them to understand our project without taking a detour through Black Jamaica, whose popularity in France and throughout the world owes much to Bob Marley and the Wailers.

To be done with the burden of race

It is perhaps the combination of all these instances I have just described that constitutes the burden of race. This term, borrowed from feminist thought, is practical. It helps us understand the stakes. For the feminist question, at least when it implicates a certain type of woman, is more acceptable and more accepted than the race question. So be it! We agree to take our umpteenth detour, to first evoke something known and familiar in order to get to something that is familiar but deliberately ignored. We can accept this as a given. But this at once imposed and indispensable detour is tiresome. It weighs heavily. This endless detour is costly to some while, quite logically, it benefits others. For as unfavorably racialized people, we assume the exhausting task of explaining, translating, and rendering intelligible situations that are violent, discriminatory, or racist. Our responsibility is double: endure, and then delicately find a happy resolution to the aggressions and injustices we have suffered – both big and small. As unfavorably racialized people, we are called on to manage and to reassure the dominant class and its members. That is to say, the dominated, the minority are called on to not make a big deal about their subalternity so as not to bother the dominant class and its members. And even when discussions about this inequality take place, the dominant group must be able to hold on to its sense of comfort, its privilege, its centrality. The comfort enjoyed by the dominant group must be maintained at all costs, notably by imposing silence. But enough already. This has to be the last detour. This effort to explain has to be the final one. Because explanations and demonstrations have been furnished and provided consistently for centuries. What is there left to understand? What remains so difficult to grasp?

It is certainly advisable to return to the most basic principles and precepts. Although it is a fiction, once race has been inscribed on the body it determines social, political, and economic relations. As such, race does exist. It has existed for centuries. It rages and is deployed on individual, communal, structural, and institutional levels. It is organized and sustained. It constitutes the negation of individuals assessed uniquely through the prism of the group they ostensibly belong to. Moreover, racism morphs according to a particular time and place. It can be anchored in the body, but can also function on a social or religious basis. It is perpetrated and endured. As a result, racism amounts to a form of violence that simultaneously affects several different types of people in any given society: those who suffer because of it and those who benefit from it, directly or indirectly. This violence is magnified tenfold by the denial of the very existence of racism. This list may be striking in the obviousness of its content. This list should amount to no more than a string of commonplaces, platitudes, truisms, and statements of fact. In Hexagonal France, in the twenty-first century, however, that simply is not the case. As such, we are well within our rights to ask whether we are dealing with a powerful form of denial or with disavowal. If it is simply a matter of denial, one wonders what kind of pathological irresponsibility has prevented a coming to consciousness. But if it is a matter of disavowal, which seems far more likely to me, then we are talking about a conscious rejection of reality. The essential question is, then, to know what is hidden behind the relentless and determined denial and rejection of the reality of race. What, that is, is the point of refusing race? This relentless denial and rejection of reality is what exposes the very stakes of that reality. This relentless and determined denial and rejection of the reality of race reveals the relations of power and the privileges at play with respect to processes of racialization. Some might offer the lazy and facile answer that, since World War II, the denial of race serves to guarantee justice and equality, all the while protecting against new discriminatory and genocidal excesses. It is a simple matter to counter such arguments with a turn to history and to the chronology of horrors perpetrated by the French nation-state: those horrors did not begin during the twentieth century. They were not limited to Hexagonal or European territories. As such, it is time to leave the Hexagon – to consider the Triangle, and the rest of the world.

Conclusion

The Orbs are Black, or, What Beauty Owes to Chaos

"I'd sing so much better
I'd dance so much better
I'd be a little free-er
A little less mean
A little less mean
A little less bitter
One day I thought I could fly
One day I woke up and I could fly
I looked down at the sea
And I wouldn't know myself
I'd have new hands
I'd have new feet
I'd have new visions"
– Nina Simone, "I wish I knew how it would feel to be free"[1]

Because this writing emerges from the Hexagon, my position differs somewhat from the invaluable reflection offered by Martinican writer Patrick Chamoiseau on the theme of writing in a "dominated country." My Black identity, in the Hexagonal context, puts me in the position of a dominated person in a dominant country. The nuance is one of scale, and it implies the need to "create dangerously," according to the phrase borrowed by Haitian-American writer Edwidge Danticat from Albert Camus. This call to "create dangerously" brings us to the indispensable tool that is subversion. Subversion through refusal. It happens by opposing the deafening silence and toxic denial. It happens through the use of the pronoun "I." So I am advocating for a form of unabashed solipsism. I consider my being, its sensations and its feelings, as constitutive of the only existing reality I can be sure of. My being, the life I have lived, my experiences constitute the foundations of my legitimacy and my authority. No one can speak in my place.

The position I occupy, specifically, is also that of a class defector. Bound up in questions of race and gender, this status can create tensions vis-à-vis my original communities. This status also sheds light on conflicts around loyalty – conflicts that must be understood alongside a feeling of betrayal. The betrayal of familial, communal, and social values and all the losses, schisms, and renunciations this betrayal has produced. Do I have the right to turn my back? On whom and on what? In what way? The desire for emancipation, be it individual or collective, must not be confused with the desire for "civilization." We must always be wary of all forms of paternalism. And so, what language can possibly express this level of complexity? What language can translate this contemporary Black French Hexagonal experience? I do not know how to answer all these questions that haunt and inhabit me still. The goal of this work has been simply to state publicly my Afro-diasporic trajectory. An *Africana* trajectory – to write, describe, and decipher this trajectory in a manner most faithful to my reality. And to do this without doubting my own expertise on the subject. For my expertise is the fruit of a lengthy international education, consistently corroborated by my own experience.

It seems to me that the question of the burden of race is central to dealing with current French society. In effect, it is time to look into the wages and the costs engendered by this socio-racial structure. Whatever the means it deploys to transform and reinvent itself, the preservation of white comfort is no longer viable. But it is no longer uniquely a question of racial domination. A truly intersectional analysis is required. Let us save some time by looking simultaneously at how race, social class, gender, and sexuality overlap and function as an ensemble. Treating each of these factors one after the other is a complete waste of time. Denying the effects of any one of these factors can only lead to an impasse.

One of the questions we must face is that of accepting an indigenization of the question of blackness in the space of the Hexagon – and in Europe, for that matter. Black identity can no longer be taken up solely through the prism of exteriority and alterity. For history has made it such that we are now speaking from the interior. This is, in fact, an uncomfortable position, inasmuch as we find ourselves, to a degree, both victims of and complicit with the executioner. That is, whatever suffering we have endured on French soil, we have benefited indirectly from France's imperialist and neo-colonial policies overseas. And sometimes these policies affect the countries our parents and ancestors come from. Moreover, this at once French, European, and Western indigenous identity has made us – *malgré nous*, "against our will"[2] – into a new type of being. Which compels us to try, no doubt vainly, not to benefit too greatly from this privileged status. In effect, we find ourselves bearing the guilty burden of "passing for white" in the eyes of our parents, of our family members still "in the old country," and of all those from the old country who have arrived more recently. That is probably who we are, albeit perhaps in some ambivalent, even diminished way.

For the last 15 years in Hexagonal France, many anti-racist figures and organizations have often found themselves described and decried as "political" by the media, by institutions, and by the political class. This label both upsets and worries me, especially when I line it up with the other catch-all label that encompasses all manner of veiled Muslims, bearded Muslims, real or supposed members of ISIS or other terrorist organizations that identify as Islamic – an ensemble, that is, of people and groups that pose a problem for the Republic. So-called "political" anti-racist organizations, judged to be identitarian and communitarian – that is, "indigenist" – are decried and accused of undermining national cohesion. By calling attention to the guilty silences and omissions from the national narrative, as it is feted and taught, these people and groups highlight the fracturing of our current society. That is one point of view. Another point of view might consist of taking into account, truly and sincerely, the theories that have been elaborated, the analyses that have been carried out, and the reports that have been established by these very organizations and people.

In addition, the question of racialization is important and concerns the whole of society, insofar as all of its components are affected and play a role in this process. Because race exists for everyone: in reality, it is a matter of seeing oneself favorably or unfavorably racialized. To put it in schematic terms, Blacks do not exist without whites. Let us quickly understand that point so as to delve into the meanders and complexities of intersectionality. Racial categorization is only one of several components of the social system produced by the West. The anti-racist struggle must then be waged by means of practices that rely on the body and on lived experience, because racist violence acts on bodies and lived experiences. Reading and listening to this new generation of anti-racists should be the very least we can do. Systematically disqualifying them is precisely a matter of racism. Lastly, one of the arguments frequently brandished by the leaders of this coordinated effort to denounce the people and organizations that are supposedly responsible for undermining the so readily invoked "we're all in this together" doctrine demands that we "move on" and "stop dwelling on the past." This argument does not hold water, for the past is systematically summoned precisely as justification for the present. The past, moreover, explains the present.

What's past is prologue.[3]

Thus, the vision of France constantly put forward is that of a secular nation, holder of specific fundamental values and traditions whose antiquity constitutes the bedrock of its legitimacy. We, too, are leaning on that French past, only our version is critical, radically different, and, above all, expanded. And we grant ourselves the right to do so because France is our home. Whether the country accepts that or not. This nationality is not an achievement. Nor is it a demand. This belonging to the French nation is not a diploma, nor even a reward or a point of pride: it is simply a matter of fact.

As such, in light of the pages and sentences presented here: I have decided to be Black.

Because I am already so plainly identified and treated as such. It is a question for me not of putting an end to denial, but of disavowal. For it is the latter that makes plain the hidden political dimension: the hierarchization, the absurd, arbitrary, and baseless categorization, the privileges, the processes of racialization, sources of all exclusions and inequalities.

I have decided to be Black. Not in the way history has defined and fashioned me on the basis of my body.

I am Black in the way that bodies like mine have reacted, battled, contested, resisted, and escaped the longstanding, repeated, and organized attempts at inferiorization. In this resistance and these affirmations of their humanity, bodies and minds that have been constructed as Black have offered the world a multitude of treasures.

I define myself as Black on my own terms – precisely in light of history. This is a matter of choice.

Through my conscious entry into a transnational community defined by its literary and artistic production, its spiritual practices, and its firm anchoring in the intellectual traditions I have evoked throughout this work, I present an act of political solidarity. In doing so, I enact what is likely a simple and oft-repeated reactualization of Negritude.

Because we invent nothing.

This leads me to ask the following questions. Since 1619 and the arrival of the first Africans, destined to be enslaved in the Jamestown colony of Virginia, at the time still British but soon to be American; since 1939 and Aimé Césaire's brilliant *Notebook*, fruit of that poet-politician's Martinican, Parisian, and Croatian peregrinations – what has happened at the heart of this Triangle and in this Hexagon? Or rather, what has not happened?

Notes

Translator's note

1 Frantz Fanon, *Peau noir, masques blancs* (Paris: Éditions du Seuil, 1952): 50. "Parler une langue, c'est assumer un monde, une culture."

Foreword

1 Dionne Brand, *An Autobiography of the Autobiography of Reading* (Alberta: University of Alberta Press, 2020): 8.
2 VeVe Clark, "Developing Diaspora Literacy and Marassa Consciousness," in Hortense Spillers, ed. *Comparative American Identities* (New York: Routledge, 1991): 40–61.
3 Katherine McKittrick and Clyde Woods, *Black Geographies and the Politics of Place* (Boston, MA: South End Press, 2007).
4 Audre Lorde, "The Master's Tools Will Never Dismantle the Master's House," in *Sister Outsider: Essays and Speeches* (Berkeley, CA: Crossing Press, 1984).
5 Brent Edwards, *The Practice of Diaspora: Literature, Translation and the Rise of Black Internationalism*

(Cambridge, MA: Harvard University Press, 2003): 13–15, 20.

6 Christina Sharpe, *In the Wake: On Blackness and Being* (Durham, NC: Duke University Press, 2016).

7 Edouard Glissant, *Caribbean Discourse*, tr. Michael Dash (Charlottesville, VA: University of Virginia Press, 1981).

8 Edwards, *The Practice of Diaspora*: 23, 24.

9 Glissant, *Caribbean Discourse*: 20. Translation modified by Brent Edwards.

10 Tina Campt, *Listening to Images* (Durham, NC: Duke University Press, 2017).

11 Alexander Weheliye, *Habeas Viscus: Racializing Assemblages, Biopolitics and Black Feminist Theories of the Human* (Durham, NC: Duke University Press, 2014).

12 NourbeSe Philip, "Discourse on the Logic of Language," in *She Tries Her Tongue, Her Silence Softly Breaks* (Middletown, CT: Wesleyan University Press, 2015).

Introduction: Black Speech/Speaking Blackness

1 A term used figuratively to designate metropolitan France, a reference to its loosely six-sided shape.

2 Trans. note: the Battle of Diên Biên Phu was a decisive battle in the First Indochina War (1954) fought between the French and the Viet Minh communist revolutionaries.

3 Created in May 1976, the Movement of Black Women is an organization of African and West Indian women students, intellectuals, and exiles dedicated to anti-colonialist feminist struggle across the Pan-African diaspora. http://musea. univ-angers.fr/exhibits/show/immigrees-exilees-femmes/ la-coordination-des-femmes-noi (last accessed January 2021).

4 A reference to Mame-Fatou Niang and Kaytie Nielsen's 2017 documentary film *Mariannes noires*, which features seven women who discuss their experience of being Black and French, *Black in France*.

5 France's overseas departments and territories, or DOM-TOM, are formerly colonial territorial authorities that have been integrated into the French Republic in the same capacity as

the departments and regions of metropolitan France. The departments consist of Martinique, Guadeloupe, French Guiana, Reunion Island, and Mayotte.

6 Yaa Gyasi, *Homegoing* (New York: Vintage Books, 2016): 295–6.

1. The Triangle

1 Gloria Hull, Patricia Bell Scott, and Barbara Smith (eds.), *All the Women Are White, All the Blacks Are Men, But Some of Us Are Brave: Black Women's Studies* (New York: Feminist Press, 1982).

2 This work was translated into French as *Black Rage. A Letter to My Son* (Paris: Autrement, 2016). Inexplicably, this translation betrays the work's premises and deprives its readers of the lyrical beauty of Richard Wright's poem "Between the World and Me," which inspired the title of Ta-Nehisi Coates's essay. In effect, Wright's poem describes his accidental discovery of the vestiges of the site of a lynching, which symbolizes the unspeakable violence enacted or endured, and thus represents the void separating white America from Black America. In doing so, this poem emphasizes the feelings of identification, contamination, and, above all, fear and terror that emerge in the face of such extreme and arbitrary violence. The French title of Coates's essay merely highlights a feeling of rage that is in fact absent from Richard Wright's poem. The interpretation suggested by the French translation thus appears completely random. It certainly would have been necessary to further consider the long African-American intellectual tradition and the genealogy of its modes of expression – notably, the foundational thinking of W.E.B. Dubois, whose first chapter in *The Souls of Black Folk* (1903) begins: "Between me and the other world there is ever an unasked question." This major work by Du Bois was translated into French by the scholar Magali Bessone as: *Les âmes du peuple noir* (Paris: Rue d'Ulm Presses de l'École normale supérieure, 2004), and republished in 2007 by La Découverte.

3 Edward W. Saïd, *Beginnings: Intention and Method* (New York: Basic Books, 1975).

4 We must, however, take note of an abolitionist literary tradition that has taken up the task of gathering the stories of enslaved Africans who survived the Middle Passage, the transatlantic voyage aboard slave ships. One of the best known of these voices is that of Olaudah Quiano, also known as Gustavus Vassa. He is the author of *The Interesting Narrative of the Life of Olaudah Equiano, or Gustavus Vassa, the African. Written by Himself.* The original publication date of this narrative is 1789.

5 Saidiya Hartman, *Lose Your Mother: A Journey Along the Atlantic Slave Route* (New York: Farrar, Straus & Giroux, 2007): 130.

6 Ibid.: 115.

7 Ruth Simms Hamilton, "Rethinking the African Diaspora: Global Dynamic," in Ruth Simms Hamilton, ed. *Routes of Passage: Rethinking the African Diaspora I* (East Lansing, MI: Michigan State University Press, 2007): 1–40.

2. University Trajectory

1 Lunatic, album *Mauvais Oeil* [Evil Eye], 45 Scientific, 2000.

2 It is important to clarify this term. In effect, there has existed a Pan-Africanist movement, the ensemble of people and institutions that organized several congresses across the world over the course of the twentieth century and that actively fought for the independence of European colonies in Africa as well as for the creation of the Organization of African Unity in 1963 (since transformed into the African Union, of which the diaspora officially became the sixth member region in 2003). It is also important to take into consideration the wide range of projects that might be described as "Pan-African," all of which have as their objective the return to Africa of Black Americans and the whole of the diaspora, along with anyone who has fought in different ways for the "elevation" of the African continent and the Black race. On this subject, see Brent Hayes Edwards's article, "The Uses of Diaspora," *Social Text* 66 (19.1) (2001): 45–73. For a purely historical approach to Pan-Africanism, see Amzat Boukari-Yabar's recent work,

Africa Unite! Une histoire du panafricanisme (Paris: La Découverte, 2014).

3 Trans. note: Direction départementale d'action sanitaire et sociale (DDAS).

4 W.E.B. Dubois, *The Souls of Black Folks*, op. cit.

5 Trans. note: Sibeth Ndiaye is a French-Senegalese communications advisor and was a government spokesperson under former French Prime Minister Édouard Philippe.

6 Colin Palmer, "Defining and studying the modern African diaspora," *The Journal of Negro History* 85.1–2 (2000): 27–32.

3. The Hexagon

1 Despo Rutti, "Frelos," *Les sirènes du charbon* [Sirens of Coal], Soldat Sans Grade, 2006. The original lyrics on the track, "Aux grands MCs, la banlieue sera toujours reconnaissante," allude to the inscription on the walls of the Pantheon in Paris, "Aux grands hommes, la patrie reconnaissante."

2 Ideal J, *Le combat continue*, Alariana/Arsenal Records, Barclay/PolyGram, 1998.

3 Ministère A.M.E.R., *95200*, Musidisc, 1994.

4 Trans. note: A reference to Martinican director and writer Euzhan Palcy's *A Dry, White Season* (1989).

5 La Rumeur, *Premier volet, Le Poison d'avril* [First Segment, April Fool], FUAS Music, 1997.

6 Trans. note: *verlan* is a form of French slang wherein the syllables of individual words are transposed to create new words with the same meaning, not unlike the structuring of Pig Latin.

7 Casey, *Tragédie d'une trajectoire* [Tragedy of a Trajectory], Dooeen Damage/Anfalsh, 2006.

8 I want to thank Tana de Soumangourou for having brought this crucial point to my attention.

9 Ministère A.M.E.R., "Sacrifice de poulets," original soundtrack for *La Haine* [Hatred], music inspired by the film, *Delabel*, 1995.

10 Ibid.

11 Suprême NTM, "Qu'est-ce qu'on attend," *Paris sous les bombes* [Paris under the Bombs] album, Epic, 1995.

12 Maboula Soumahoro, "On the test of the French Republic as taken (and failed)," *Transition* 98 (2008): 42–66.

13 Trans. note: École des hautes études en sciences sociales (EHESS).

14 Trica D. Keaton, *Muslim Girls and the Other France: Race, Identity Politics, and Social Exclusion* (Bloomington, IN: Indiana University Press, 2006).

15 Refers to the decolonial grassroots organization that emerged in 2005 to address structural racism in France.

16 Trans note: Conseil représentatif des associations noires de France (Cran).

17 Sandrine Lemaire, Nicolas Bancel, and Pascal Blanchard (eds.), *La Fracture coloniale. La société française au prisme de l'héritage colonial* (Paris: La Découverte, 2006).

18 Éric Fassin and Didier Fassin (eds.), *De la question sociale à la question raciale? Représenter la société française* (Paris: La Découverte, 2006).

19 Pap Ndiaye, *La Condition noire. Essai sur une minorité française* (Paris: Calmann-Lévy, 2008).

20 This thesis has, however, been freely available on the Internet since 2008.

21 Term used to designate those whose gender assignment at birth corresponds to their actual gender identity.

22 My approach consists of bringing to light what constitutes the system; it is not a matter of naming those I have mentioned throughout this work. However, given the lack of recognition they are met with most often in the Hexagonal context, I will go ahead and name Martinican deputy Serge Letchimy. He is the author of a decisive thesis on urbanism, presented at the Sorbonne, and inspiration for the character of the "urbanist" in Patrick Chamoiseau's dazzling novel *Texaco*, which received the Goncourt Prize in 1992, 70 years after René Maran and his novel *Batouala*. So much things to say, yes … [Trans. note: A reference to the title of Bob Marley's 1993 track].

23 "Question au gouvernement numéro 3926" [Question number 3926 for the government], http://questions. assemblee-nationale.fr/q13/13-3926QG.htm, "L'intégralité

de la question du député Letchimy sur les propos de M. Guéant" [The full question posed by Deputy Letchimy concerning Mr. Guéant's statements], LeMonde.fr, February 7, 2012, www.lemonde.fr/election-presidentielle-2012/article/2012/02/07/l-integralite-de-la-question-du-depute-letchimy-sur-les-propos-de-m-gueant_1640097_1471069.html.

24 Aimé Césaire, *Discourse on Colonialism* (Paris: Présence Africaine, 1955).

25 Three French expatriate women in New York: Rachida Naceur, Namisata Soumahoro, and Jennifer Tchiakpe.

26 Bob Marley and the Wailers, *Survival*, Island Records/Tuff Gong, 1979.

Conclusion: The Orbs are Black, or, What Beauty Owes to Chaos

1 Improvisation on an original song during a concert. The video is accessible via the following link: www.youtube.com/watch?v=N4CbuE6--as.

2 Trans. note: The term *malgré-nous* refers to men of the contested Alsace-Moselle region who found themselves conscripted into the German Wehrmacht or the Waffen-SS during World War II.

3 I cite William Shakespeare's play, *The Tempest* (1610 or 1611), keeping in mind the adaptation and fundamental critique proposed by Aimé Césaire in 1969 in *A Tempest*.

Index

Notes are indicated by the use of 'n'.